Daily
Fellowship
with
God

Daily
Fellowship
with
God

LARRY W. WILSON

HERALD PRESS
Scottdale, Pennsylvania
Waterloo, Ontario

Library of Congress Cataloging-in-Publication
Data
Wilson, Larry W., 1936-
    Daily fellowship with God / Larry W. Wilson.
        p.   cm.
    ISBN 0-8361-3595-4 (alk. paper)
    1. Devotional calendars.   2. Prayer-books.
I. Title.
BV4811.W5925   1992
242'.8—dc20
                                92-20247
                                CIP

The paper used in this publication is recycled
and meets the minimum requirements of American National Standard for Information Sciences
—Permanence of Paper for Printed Library Mate-
rials, ANSI Z39.48-1984.

See pages 13-14 for Scripture credits.

DAILY FELLOWSHIP WITH GOD
Copyright © 1992 by Herald Press, Scottdale,
    Pa. 15683
    Published simultaneously in Canada by
    Herald Press, Waterloo, Ont. N2L 6H7
    All rights reserved
Library of Congress Catalog Card Number:
    92-20247
International Standard Book Number:
    0-8361-3595-4
Printed in the United States of America
Cover and book design by Gwen M. Stamm

99 98 97 96 95   10 9 8 7 6 5 4 3

*To Myrtle Kern Thomas,
my mother-in-law,
whose testimony
helped me enjoy
fellowship with God*

*W*hat we have seen and heard
we announce to you also,
so that you join with us
in the fellowship that we have
with the Father and
with his Son Jesus Christ.

—*1 John 1:3, TEV*

Contents

Foreword

E ver since Norman Vincent Peale intro-
duced his concept of "positive thinking" some years ago, scores of contempo-
rary writers have offered their formulas for
achieving success, happiness, and a sense
of purpose in everyday living. It is primarily
a matter, they tell us, of thinking positive
thoughts with regular deliberation, while
refusing to dwell on the endless array of
negatives that can so insidiously occupy the
mind.

We grant that there is no magic in such
an approach. Yet the premise is a sound
one—and for a very good reason. The idea
originated, not with late-twentieth-century
psychologists, but with the Word of God.

Remember: "Finally, beloved, whatever
is true, whatever is honorable, whatever is
just, whatever is pure, whatever is pleasing,
whatever is commendable, if there is any
excellence and if there is anything worthy
of praise, think about these things" (Phil.
4:8, NRSV).

There has never been any psychotherapy
as powerful and as effectual as that given to
us long ago in Scripture. Larry Wilson is
vitally aware of this great truth as he
presents to the reader these timeless posi-
tives to be drawn one day at a time from the

arsenal of God's eternal answers to human troubles. "Let us fight back," he prescribes, "by saturating our conscious and subconscious minds with praise, hope, thanksgiving, and Scripture."

Surely, that is the path to a genuine daily fellowship with God. This unique collection of devotional readings, with its simplified, consistent outline for each day's meditation, is destined to bring comfort and spiritual growth to many thousands of Christians who seek a closer walk with their blessed Lord.

—D. James Kennedy, Senior Minister
Coral Ridge Presbyterian Church
Fort Lauderdale, Florida

Preface

The mind is a battleground where Satan attacks Christians with an arsenal of negative, discouraging thoughts to keep us from enjoying God's fellowship and abundant living. These destructive forces bombard us from every direction. If left unchallenged, they wreak havoc on our bodies, souls, and spirits.

God has given us power to choose the thoughts we think—but there is a problem. Selecting positive, constructive thoughts takes effort and self-discipline.

The easy way is to wallow in negative thought patterns: resentments, discouragement, self-pity, self-blame. These distort our perceptions and rob us of peace with God.

The purpose of this resource is to offer one solution to the dilemma. Let us deliberately program our minds with daily constructive input. This can be our conscious effort to "take every thought captive and make it obey Christ" (2 Cor. 10:5, TEV).

This book is small by design so it can be easily carried and instantly produced. If we need to deal with guilt, want an inspirational lift, or feel ourselves being seduced by negative emotions, disturbing thoughts, defeatist attitudes, or destructive feelings—assistance is at our fingertips.

With this book, we can fill our hearts with praise and be assured of God's presence. We can be challenged by God's Word to obey rather than mope or rebel. We can experience the guidance of the Holy Spirit by setting daily goals and exercising our faith. We can express our gratitude and bolster our hope by meditating on God's promises.

For victorious living, stability, and mutual encouragement, let us also not neglect to meet regularly with other Christians. Yet even when alone, with Jesus we can say, "Go away, Satan!" (Matt. 4:10, TEV), and make space for the Lord to commune with us through our minds and spirits.

Fellowship is hindered, however, or even completely disrupted if we allow destructive feelings, emotions, thoughts, attitudes and/or moods to sap our energy and drag us down emotionally and spiritually.

Instead, let us fight back by saturating our conscious and subconscious minds with praise, hope, thanksgiving, Scripture, and hymns. In so doing, we assure ourselves of uplifting, daily, continuing faith-building fellowship with God the Father, the Son, and the Holy Spirit.

—*Larry W. Wilson, Pastor*
Grace United Methodist Church
Coal Center, Pennsylvania

Scripture Credits

Scripture is excerpted from the verses named, used by permission with all rights reserved, and identified by abbreviations:

JB   *The Jerusalem Bible*, copyright ©
       1966 by Darton, Longman & Todd,
       Ltd., and Doubleday, a division of
       Bantam, Doubleday, Dell Publish-
       ing Group, Inc.

KJV   *The King James Version*

NASB   *The New American Standard Bible*,
       © The Lockman Foundation 1960,
       1962, 1963, 1968, 1971, 1972, 1973,
       1975.

NEB   *The New English Bible*, © The
       Delegates of the Oxford University
       Press and the Syndics of the Cam-
       bridge University Press 1961, 1970.

NIV   *The New International Version*,
       copyright © 1973, 1978, 1984 Inter-
       national Bible Society, by permis-
       sion of Zondervan Bible Publishers.

NKJB   *The New King James Bible*,
       copyright 1979, 1980, 1982,
       Thomas Nelson, Inc., Publishers.

NRSV   *The New Revised Standard Version*,
       copyright 1989, by the Division of

Users of *Daily Fellowship with God* are
encouraged to read chapters and books in
the Bible. This will supply additional spiritual nourishment and aid in seeking God's
glory.

Bible Book Names

In alphabetical order, the following abbreviations are used:

Chron. — Chronicles
Col. — Colossians
Cor. — Corinthians
Dan. — Daniel
Deut. — Deuteronomy
Eccles. — Ecclesiastes
Eph. — Ephesians
Exod. — Exodus
Ezek. — Ezekiel
Gal. — Galatians
Gen. — Genesis
Hab. — Habakkuk
Hag. — Haggai
Heb. — Hebrews
Hos. — Hosea
Isa. — Isaiah
Jas. — James
Jer. — Jeremiah
Jon. — Jonah
Josh. — Joshua
Judg. — Judges
Lev. — Leviticus
Mal. — Malachi
Matt. — Matthew
Mic. — Micah
Neh. — Nehemiah
Num. — Numbers
Pet. — Peter

Phil. — Philippians
Prov. — Proverbs
Ps. — Psalms
Rev. — Revelation
Rom. — Romans
Sam. — Samuel
Thess. — Thessalonians
Tim. — Timothy
Zech. — Zechariah
Zeph. — Zephaniah

January 1

Praise

Bless the Lord, O my soul:
    and all that is within me,
        bless his holy name.

Ps. 103:1, KJV

Proposal

Don't be anxious about tomorrow. God will take care of your tomorrow too. Live one day at a time.

Matt. 6:34, TLB

Practice

Today I'll think only hopeful thoughts. My focus will be solely on the Lord Jesus.

Promise

The thief comes only in order to steal, kill, and destroy. I have come in order that you might have life—life in all its fullness.

John 10:10, TEV

Prayer

Thank you, Lord, for entering my heart and enabling me to experience life in abundance. Amen.

Praise

Let all those that seek thee
     rejoice and be glad in thee:
and let such as love thy salvation say
          continually,
     Let God be magnified.

Ps. 70:4, KJV

Proposal

Just as you trusted Christ to save you, trust
him, too, for each day's problems; live in
vital union with him.

Col. 2:6, TLB

Practice

Today I'll trust the Lord in every circumstance, without exception.

Promise

I will instruct you (says the Lord) and guide
you along the best pathway for your life; I
will advise you and watch your progress.

Ps. 32:8, TLB

Prayer

Thank you, Lord, for the guidance, counsel,
and instruction you offer to me every day.
Amen.

January 3

Praise

I will praise thee [O Lord] with my
  whole heart:
before the gods will I sing praise unto thee.

Ps. 138:1, KJV

Proposal

Base your happiness on your hope in
Christ. When trials come endure them
patiently; steadfastly maintain the habit of
prayer.

Rom. 12:12, Phillips

Practice

Today I'll focus on Christ, look upon trials as
opportunities for growth, and pray for
patience.

Promise

The Lord is close to the brokenhearted and
saves those who are crushed in spirit.

Ps. 34:18, NIV

Prayer

Thank you, Lord, for being with me when
I'm brokenhearted and for being a source
of comfort in times of stress. Amen.

Praise

Who is like thee, O Lord, among the gods?
Who is like thee, majestic in holiness,
  terrible in glorious deeds, doing wonders?

Exod. 15:11, RSV

Proposal

Don't be afraid, for the Lord will go before
you and will be with you; he will not fail nor
forsake you.

Deut. 31:8, TLB

Practice

Today I refuse to be intimidated by fear. I'll
immediately dispel any such notion.

Promise

Remember, I will be with you and protect
you wherever you go. . . . I will not leave
you until I have done all that I have
promised you.

Gen. 28:15, TEV

Prayer

Thank you, Lord, for your protection
wherever I go. Amen.

January 5

Praise

Come, everyone, and clap for joy!
   Shout triumphant praises to the Lord!
For the Lord, the God above all gods,
   is awesome beyond words;
he is the great King of all the earth.

Ps. 47:1-2, TLB

Proposal

Commit your work to the Lord,
   and your plans will be established.

Prov. 16:3, RSV

Practice

Today I'll commit my labor to the glory of
God and trust him to satisfy my needs.

Promise

Behold, I send the promise of my Father
upon you; but stay in the city, until you are
clothed with power from on high.

Luke 24:49, RSV

Prayer

Thank you, Lord, for your Spirit, who
empowers, guides, and comforts me in all
the happenings of life. Amen.

January 6

Praise

[The wise men] saw the child with Mary his
mother, and they fell down and worshiped
him. . . . They offered him gifts, gold and
frankincense and myrrh.

Matt. 2:11, RSV

Proposal

Do not be anxious about anything, but in
everything, by prayer and petition, with
thanksgiving, present your requests to God.

Phil. 4:6, NIV

Practice

Today I'll allow no negative image to dwell
in my mind; I'll think only positive
thoughts.

Promise

The peace of God, which transcends all
understanding, will guard your hearts and
your minds in Christ Jesus.

Phil. 4:7, NIV

Prayer

Thank you, Lord, for flooding my soul with
perfect peace. Amen.

January 7

Praise

For great is the Lord and most worthy
    of praise;
    he is to be feared above all gods.

1 Chron. 16:25, NIV

Proposal

Do not love the world or the things in the
world. If any one loves the world, love for
the Father is not in him.

1 John 2:15, RSV

Practice

Today I refuse to lust after power, money,
fame, or anything of this world.

Promise

In [Christ] we have redemption through his
blood, the forgiveness of our trespasses,
according to the riches of his grace.

Eph. 1:7, RSV

Prayer

Thank you, Lord, for shedding your precious blood, giving me salvation, and
forgiving my sins. Amen.

Praise

I will give to the Lord the thanks due
    to his righteousness,
    and I will sing praise to the name of
    the Lord, the Most High.

Ps. 7:17, RSV

Proposal

Go, therefore, make disciples of all the
nations; baptize them . . . and teach them.

Matt. 28:19-20, JB

Practice

Today I'll be sensitive to the leading of the
Holy Spirit; I'll witness for Christ as
opportunities arise.

Promise

In keeping with his promise we are looking
forward to a new heaven and a new earth,
the home of righteousness.

2 Pet. 3:13, NIV

Prayer

Thank you, Lord, for the promise of a new
earth where evil will be no more. Amen.

Praise

O Lord, thou art my God;
I will exalt thee, I will praise thy name;
    for thou hast done wonderful things.

Isa. 25:1, RSV

Proposal

Seek first [God's] kingdom and his
righteousness, and all these things shall be
yours as well.

Matt. 6:33, RSV

Practice

Today I'll be obedient and dependent upon
the Lord Jesus Christ and allow nothing to
divert me from these objectives.

Promise

Blessed is anyone who endures temptation.
Such a one . . . will receive the crown of life
that the Lord has promised to those who
love him.

Jas. 1:12, NRSV

Prayer

Thank you, Lord, for the crown of life I'll
receive one day. Amen.

January 10

Praise

Lord, . . . rescue me
and I will be perfectly safe.
You are the one I praise!

Jer. 17:14, TEV

Proposal

Be not wise in your own eyes;
fear the Lord and shun evil.

Prov. 3:7, NIV

Practice

Today I refuse to rely on my own wisdom.
I'll expel negative thoughts and lean on the
Lord for insight and inspiration.

Promise

If you are Christ's, then you are Abraham's
offspring, heirs according to promise.

Gal. 3:29, RSV

Prayer

Thank you, Lord, for allowing me to be your
heir. Thank you for the promises you gave
to Abraham that now apply to me. Amen.

Praise

Sing praises to the Lord,
    for he has done gloriously;
    let this be known in all the earth.

Isa. 12:5, RSV

Proposal

The end of the matter; all has been heard.
Fear God, and keep his commandments;
for that is the whole duty of everyone.

Eccles. 12:13, NRSV

Practice

Today I'll approach the Lord with reverence
and awe, praise him, and keep his commandments.

Promise

We know that in all things God works for
the good of those who love him, who have
been called according to his purpose.

Rom. 8:28, NIV

Prayer

Thank you, Lord, for the good that comes
from failures as well as successes. Amen.

Praise

Set me free from my distress;
    then . . . I will praise you
        because of your goodness to me.

Ps. 142:7, TEV

Proposal

Bring the full tithes into the storehouse, that
there may be food in my house; and thereby put me to the test, says the Lord of hosts.

Mal. 3:10, RSV

Practice

Today I'll put the Lord first in the area of
finances and place the needs of others
ahead of my own.

Promise

Put me to the test, says the Lord of hosts, if I
will not open the windows of heaven for
you and pour down for you an overflowing
blessing.

Mal. 3:10, RSV

Prayer

Thank you, Lord, for showering abundant
blessings upon me. Amen.

January 13

Praise

They shall come from the cities, . . .
bringing sacrifices of praise,
unto the house of the Lord.

Jer. 17:26, KJV

Proposal

Do not let sin control your puny body any
longer; do not give in to its sinful desires.

Rom. 6:12, TLB

Practice

Today I refuse to fall victim to Satan's lies.
I'll conduct a moral inventory and confess
any unforgiven sin.

Promise

Sin need never again be your master, for
now you are no longer tied to the law where
sin enslaves you, but you are free under
God's favor and mercy.

Rom. 6:14, TLB

Prayer

Thank you, Lord, for liberating me from the
bondage of sin. Amen.

Praise

Yours, O Lord, is the greatness and
    the power
    and the glory and the majesty and
      the splendor,
    for everything in heaven and earth
      is yours.

1 Chron. 29:11, NIV

Proposal

For freedom Christ has set us free; stand
fast therefore, and do not submit again to a
yoke of slavery.

Gal. 5:1, RSV

Practice

Today I'll experience freedom from
bondage by relying on the power of the
Holy Spirit.

Promise

If any of you is lacking in wisdom, ask God,
. . . and it will be given you.

Jas. 1:5, NRSV

Prayer

Thank you, Lord, for being accessible to me
any time of the night or day. Amen.

January 15

Praise

Praise ye the Lord.
Praise ye the Lord from the heavens:
    praise him in the heights.

Ps. 148:1, KJV

Proposal

Be strong in the Lord. Put on the full armor
of God so that you can take your stand
against the devil's schemes.

Eph. 6:10-11, NIV

Practice

Today I'll resist negative thinking in every
circumstance by being clad in the armor of
God.

Promise

The Lord your God is with you;
    his power gives you victory.
The Lord will take delight in you,
    and in his love he will give you new life.

Zeph. 3:17, TEV

Prayer

Thank you, Lord, for the zest for life your
presence affords me. Amen.

January 16

Praise

Shout aloud and sing for joy,
  people of Zion,
for great is the Holy One of Israel
  among you.

Isa. 12:6, NIV

Proposal

Can any of you by worrying add a single
hour to your span of life?

Luke 12:25, NRSV

Practice

Today I refuse to worry. If worrisome
thoughts enter my mind, I'll immediately
dispel them and turn to the Lord for
assistance.

Promise

I have called you by name—you are mine.
When you pass through deep waters,
  I will be with you;
  your troubles will not overwhelm you.

Isa. 43:1, TEV

Prayer

Thank you, Lord, for comforting me during
times of emotional upheaval. Amen.

Praise

O God ...

We your people, the flock of your pasture,
 will give thanks to you forever;
  from generation to generation
   we will recount your praise.

Ps. 79:1, 13, NRSV

Proposal

Do not be conformed to this world but be
transformed by the renewal of your mind.

Rom. 12:2, RSV

Practice

Today I refuse to be seduced by temptation.
Instead, I'll renew my mind by meditating
on the Word of God.

Promise

In my Father's house are many mansions: if
it were not so, I would have told you. I go to
prepare a place for you.

John 14:2, KJV

Prayer

Thank you, Lord, for the eternal dwelling
place you have prepared for me. Amen.

Praise

I will thank you [O God] forever,
     because of what you have done.
In the presence of the faithful
     I will proclaim your name, for it is good.

Ps. 52:9, NRSV

Proposal

For where you have envy and selfish ambition, there you find disorder and every evil practice.

Jas. 3:16, NIV

Practice

Today I'll engage in neither envy nor self-seeking. I'll be joyful for those who are richly blessed.

Promise

In Christ Jesus you are all children of God through faith.

Gal. 3:26, NRSV

Prayer

Thank you, Lord, for revealing yourself through Christ Jesus and for giving me the privilege of being your descendant. Amen.

January 19

Praise
Praise ye the Lord.
Praise God in his sanctuary:
    praise him in the firmament of his power.
Ps. 150:1, KJV

Proposal
We Christians . . . can be mirrors that
brightly reflect the glory of the Lord. And as
the Spirit of the Lord works within us, we
become more and more like him
2 Cor. 3:18, TLB

Practice
Today I'll covet the infilling of the Holy
Spirit and the Spirit's leading and guidance
in every situation.

Promise
You are no longer a slave but a child, and if
a child then also an heir, through God.
Gal. 4:7, NRSV

Prayer
Thank you, Lord, for elevating me to the
position of heir of all your riches. Amen.

January 20

Praise

When [Jesus] came near Jerusalem, . . . his disciples began to thank God and praise him in loud voices for all the great things that they had seen.

Luke 19:37, TEV

Proposal

Take courage . . . work, for I am with you, says the Lord of hosts. . . . My Spirit abides among you; fear not.

Hag. 2:4-5, RSV

Practice

Today I'll fear nothing. I'll acknowledge my weaknesses and allow the Lord to manifest his strength.

Promise

I, the Lord your God, brought you out of Egypt so that you would no longer be slaves.

Lev. 26:13, TEV

Prayer

Thank you, Lord, for liberating me from bondage, from selfishness, and from sinful passions. Amen.

January 21

Praise

The Levites and the priests praised the Lord day by day, singing with loud instruments unto the Lord.

2 Chron. 30:21, KJV

Proposal

Why am I so sad?
    Why am I so troubled?
I will put my hope in God,
    and once again I will praise him,
    my savior and my God.

Ps. 42:11, TEV

Practice

Today I refuse to focus on problems. I'll put my hope in God and praise him every time a negative thought enters my mind.

Promise

Our steps are made firm by the Lord,
    when he delights in our way.

Ps. 37:23, NRSV

Prayer

Thank you, Lord, for being my constant companion and guiding me through difficult situations. Amen.

Praise

Praise the Lord, all his works
　　everywhere in his dominion.
Praise the Lord, O my soul.

Ps. 103:22, NIV

Proposal

Happy are those
　　who do not follow the advice of
　　　　the wicked,
or take the path that sinners tread,
　　or sit in the seat of scoffers.

Ps. 1:1, NRSV

Practice

Today I refuse to grieve the Lord. I'll spend
time seeking his will and the power to carry
it out.

Promise

You will call, and the Lord will answer;
You will cry, and he will say, "Here I am."

Isa. 58:9, NASB

Prayer

Thank you, Lord, for helping me through
periods of excruciating emotional pain.
Amen.

January 23

Praise

The trumpeters and singers joined in
unison, as with one voice, to give praise
and thanks to the Lord. . . . They raised
their voices in praise to the Lord and sang:

"He is good;
his love endures forever."

2 Chron. 5:13, NIV

Proposal

Trust in the Lord God always, for in the Lord
Jehovah is your everlasting strength.

Isa. 26:4, TLB

Practice

Today I'll totally trust the Lord and make
every effort to practice patience in each
situation.

Promise

Come to me, all you who are weary and bur-
dened, and I will give you rest.

Matt. 11:28, NIV

Prayer

Thank you, Lord, for restoring my soul
during times of distress. Amen.

Praise

Praise the Lord.
Give thanks to the Lord, for he is good;
    his love endures forever.

Ps. 106:1, NIV

Proposal

If you make my word your home
you will indeed be my disciples,
you will learn the truth
and the truth will make you free.

John 8:31, JB

Practice

Today I'll give the Word of God top priority
by meditating on selected verses.

Promise

Whoever believes in me, as the Scripture
has said, streams of living water will flow
from within him.

John 7:38, NIV

Prayer

Thank you, Lord, for your Spirit, who never
sleeps and who ministers to my innermost
needs. Amen.

January 25

Praise

[Jehoshaphat] appointed those who were to
sing to the Lord and praise him in holy
splendor . . . saying:

"Give thanks to the Lord,
for his steadfast love endures forever."

2 Chron. 20:21, NRSV

Proposal

Does the Lord delight in burnt
offerings and sacrifices
as much as in obeying the voice of
the Lord?
To obey is better than sacrifice.

1 Sam. 15:22, NIV

Practice

Today I'll totally surrender myself to the
Lord and obey him without fail.

Promise

[The Lord] guides the humble in what is
right and teaches them his way.

Ps. 25:9, NIV

Prayer

Thank you, Lord, for your Word, which
lights the way to a satisfying life. Amen.

Praise

Praise the Lord, O Jerusalem!
　　Praise your God, O Zion!

Ps. 147:12, TEV

Proposal

Confess your sins to each other and pray for
each other so that you may be healed.

Jas. 5:16, NIV

Practice

I'll freely minister to the afflicted as opportunities arise. If I become ill today, I'll confess my sins and solicit the prayers of
others.

Promise

The prayer of the righteous is powerful and
effective.

Jas. 5:16, NRSV

Prayer

Thank you, Lord, for providing the gift of
righteousness through Jesus, and for the
blessings of answered prayer. Amen.

January 27

Praise

To you, O God of my ancestors,
    I give thanks and praise,
for you have given me wisdom and power.

Dan. 2:23, NRSV

Proposal

Always be full of joy in the Lord; I say it
again, rejoice!

Phil. 4:4, TLB

Practice

Lord, with the aid of this book, I'll praise
you and be glad in your presence today.

Promise

Those of steadfast mind you keep
        in peace—
    in peace because they trust in you.

Isa. 26:3, NRSV

Prayer

Thank you, Lord, for the perfect peace that
comes from trusting you. I praise you for
this precious gift, one of many priceless
treasures you offer me each day. Amen.

Praise

All praise to God for his wonderful kindness to us and his favor that he has poured out upon us, because we belong to his dearly loved Son.

Eph. 1:6, TLB

Proposal

Do not neglect to do good and to share what you have, for such sacrifices are pleasing to God.

Heb. 13:16, RSV

Practice

Today I'll be a blessing to others because of my love for the Lord.

Promise

Delight yourself in the Lord
and he will give you the desires of
your heart.

Ps. 37:4, NIV

Prayer

Thank you, Lord, for granting the desires of a heart that overflows with joy. Amen.

January 29

Praise

The Lord is my strength and my song . . .
this is my God, and I will praise him,
    my father's God, and I will exalt him.

Exod. 15:2, RSV

Proposal

Don't worry about food—what to eat and
drink; don't worry at all that God will
provide it for you.

Luke 12:29, TLB

Practice

Today I'll place my life in God's hands,
without reservation. Consequently, I have
no need to worry about the past, the future,
or the present.

Promise

Your heavenly Father . . . will always give
you all you need from day to day if you will
make the kingdom of God your primary
concern.

Luke 12:30-31, TLB

Prayer

Thank you, Lord, for satisfying my needs
one day at a time. Amen.

January 30

Praise

The Lord lives! Blessed be my rock,
and exalted be the God of my salvation.

Ps. 18:46, NRSV

Proposal

You will not have to fight this battle. Just
take up your positions and wait; you will
see the Lord give you victory. . . . Do not
hesitate or be afraid. Go out to battle, and
the Lord will be with you!

2 Chron. 20:17, TEV

Practice

With the Lord by my side, I'll be unafraid
today and be able to handle anything that
comes along.

Promise

The Lord will protect you from all danger;
he will keep you safe.
He will protect you as you come and go
now and forever.

Ps. 121:7-8, TEV

Prayer

Thank you, Lord, for being my protector
every day and throughout eternity. Amen.

January 31

Praise

I will always praise you, [Lord,]
  because you teach me your laws.
Ps. 119:171, TEV

Proposal

Beloved, whatever is true . . . honorable . . .
just . . . pure . . . pleasing . . . commendable,
if there is any excellence and if there is anything worthy of praise, think about these
things.
Phil. 4:8, NRSV

Practice

Today I'll fill my mind with thoughts that are
pure and productive, and I'll reject those
that are degrading and destructive.

Promise

I am not going to leave you alone in the
world—I am coming to you.
John 14:18, Phillips

Prayer

Thank you, Lord, for living in me, defeating
Satan, and taking fear out of death. Amen.

February 1

Praise

Praise [God] for his mighty acts;
  praise him according to his
    excellent greatness.

Ps. 150:2, KJV

Proposal

Cast all your anxieties on [God],
  for he cares about you.

1 Pet. 5:7, RSV

Practice

Today I'll surrender to the Lord and trust
him in every situation. In addition, I'll turn
over to him the regrets of yesterday and the
anxieties of tomorrow.

Promise

The Lord is my light and my salvation;
  whom shall I fear?
The Lord is the stronghold of my life;
  of whom shall I be afraid?

Ps. 27:1, RSV

Prayer

Thank you, Lord, for being my light, my salvation, and the stronghold of my life. Amen.

February 2

Praise

I, Nebuchadnezzar, lifted my eyes to heaven . . . and I blessed the Most High, and praised and honored him who lives for ever; for his dominion is an everlasting dominion.

Dan. 4:34, RSV

Proposal

Who is it that conquers the world but the one who believes that Jesus is the Son of God?

1 John 5:5, NRSV

Practice

Today I'll live my life in accordance with the way I really believe, that Jesus is the only begotten Son of God.

Promise

The Lord will guide you continually,
  and satisfy your desire with good things.

Isa. 58:11, RSV

Prayer

Thank you, Lord, for the joy of walking with you each day. Amen.

February 3

Praise
From the throne came a voice crying,
  "Praise our God, all you his servants,
  you who fear him, small and great."

Rev. 19:5, RSV

Proposal
Prepare your minds for action; be self-controlled; set your hope fully on the grace to be given you.

1 Pet. 1:13, NIV

Practice
Today I'll deal with any situation by being under the control of the Holy Spirit and motivated by the grace of God.

Promise
If anyone does sin, we have an advocate with the Father, Jesus Christ the righteous.

1 John 2:1, NRSV

Prayer
Thank you, Lord, for accepting me into your kingdom. Amen.

February 4

Praise

O Lord, our Lord,
> how majestic is your name in all the
> earth!

You have set your glory above the heavens.

Ps. 8:1, NIV

Proposal

All that is in the world, the lust of the flesh
and the lust of the eyes and the pride of life,
is not of the Father but is of the world.

1 John 2:16, RSV

Practice

Today I'll focus my thoughts upon Jesus and
acknowledge my utter dependence upon
him.

Promise

If we confess our sins, [God] is faithful and
just and will forgive us our sins and purify
us from all unrighteousness.

1 John 1:9, NIV

Prayer

Thank you, Lord, for a clear and guilt-free
conscience. Amen.

February 5

Praise

O come, let us sing unto the Lord:
    let us make a joyful noise to the
        rock of our salvation.

Ps. 95:1, KJV

Proposal

Be self-controlled and alert. Your enemy the devil prowls around like a roaring lion looking for someone to devour.

1 Pet. 5:8, NIV

Practice

Today I'll be filled with the Holy Spirit, clad in the armor of God, and covered by the supreme sacrifice of Jesus.

Promise

God so loved the world that he gave his only Son, that whoever believes in him should not perish but have eternal life.

John 3:16, RSV

Prayer

Thank you, Lord Jesus, for protecting me from the prowling devil and bringing me eternal life. Amen.

Praise

I will put my hope in God,
    and once again I will praise him,
        my savior and my God.

Ps. 42:5. TEV

Proposal

Rid yourselves of all malice and all deceit,
hypocrisy, envy, and slander of every kind.

1 Pet. 2:1, NIV

Practice

Today I'll rely on the Holy Spirit to keep me
from becoming a victim of either angry or
fearful temper.

Promise

God is able to provide you with every blessing in abundance, so that you may always
have enough of everything and may
provide in abundance for every good work.

2 Cor. 9:8, RSV

Prayer

Thank you, Lord, for the freedom to control
my thoughts, words, and actions. Amen.

February 7

Praise

May he be pleased with my song. . . .
Praise the Lord, my soul!
   Praise the Lord!

Ps. 104:34-35, TEV

Proposal

Dear friends, I urge you . . . abstain from
sinful desires, which war against your soul.

1 Pet. 2:11, NIV

Practice

Today I'll resist the urge to repress anger
and form resentments. Instead, with God's
grace I'll express my feelings by talking
them out.

Promise

In this world you will have trouble. But take
heart! I have overcome the world.

John 16:33, NIV

Prayer

Thank you, Lord, for comforting me during
seasons of personal crises. Amen.

February 8

Praise

According to thy name, O God, so is thy
praise unto the ends of the earth:
thy right hand is full of righteousness.

Ps. 48:10, KJV

Proposal

Do not be afraid or discouraged because of
this vast army. For the battle is not yours,
but God's.

2 Chron. 20:15, NIV

Practice

Today I refuse to be discouraged by the
shortcomings of others. I'll rise above
upsetting circumstances by not taking
myself too seriously.

Promise

The Lord gives wisdom,
and from his mouth come
knowledge and understanding.

Prov. 2:6, NIV

Prayer

Thank you, Lord, for all the good counsel
contained in the Bible. Amen.

February 9

Praise

In the assembly of all your people, Lord
 I told the good news
  that you save us.
You know that I will never stop
 telling it.

Ps. 40:9, TEV

Proposal

Share each other's troubles and problems,
and so obey our Lord's command.

Gal. 6:2, TLB

Practice

Today I'll share the burdens of others by
being willing to lend an ear.

Promise

Even though I walk through the valley of
  the shadow of death,
 I fear no evil; for Thou art with me;
Thy rod and Thy staff, they comfort me.

Ps. 23:4, NASB

Prayer

Thank you, Lord, for your Spirit, who leads
me in the way of love and casts out fear.
Amen.

February 10

Praise

The Lord is king forever.

Your God, O Zion, will reign for all time.
Praise the Lord!

Ps. 146:10, TEV

Proposal

Happy are those who are concerned for
the poor;
the Lord will help them when they are
in trouble.

Ps. 41:1, TEV

Practice

Today I'll approach the downtrodden with
respect and compassion by remembering
that, but for the grace of God, there go I.

Promise

Those who trust in the Lord are steady as
Mount Zion, unmoved by any circumstance. . . . The Lord surrounds and protects
his people.

Ps. 125: 1-2, TLB

Prayer

Thank you, Lord, for being my refuge in
times of trouble. Amen.

Praise

Praise God, O heaven and earth,
   seas and all creatures in them.

Ps. 69:34, TEV

Proposal

Always be ready to make your defense to
anyone who demands from you an ac-
counting for the hope that is in you.

1 Pet. 3:15, NRSV

Practice

Today I'll tell anyone who will listen, in the
most gentle way possible, why I trust Christ
in all things.

Promise

If they fall, they will not stay down,
   because the Lord will help them up.

Ps. 37:24, TEV

Prayer

Thank you, Lord, for uplifting me spiritually
and emotionally when I stumble and fall.
Amen.

February 12

Praise

At the name of Jesus every knee should
>   bow, . . .
and every tongue confess that Jesus Christ
>   is Lord,
>   to the glory of God the Father.

Phil. 2:10-11, NIV

Proposal

Love is very patient and kind, never jealous
or envious, never boastful or proud.

1 Cor. 13:4, TLB

Practice

Today, if greed or any other temptation
enters my thoughts, I'll overcome with the
Lord's help.

Promise

I will turn their mourning into gladness;
>   I will give them comfort and joy instead
>   of sorrow.

Jer. 31:13, NIV

Prayer

Thank you, Lord, for using others to comfort me during seasons of suffering. Amen.

Praise

O Jehovah, our Lord,
  the majesty and glory of your name
    fills the earth.

Ps. 8:9, TLB

Proposal

Keep your conscience clear, so that, when
you are abused, those who revile your good
behavior in Christ may be put to shame.

1 Pet. 3:16, RSV

Practice

Today I refuse to do anything that might
jeopardize my fellowship with the Lord.

Promise

I am convinced that neither death, nor life,
nor angels, nor rulers, nor things present,
nor things to come, nor powers, nor height,
nor depth, nor anything else in all creation,
will be able to separate us from the love of
God in Christ Jesus our Lord.

Rom. 8:38-39, NRSV

Prayer

Thank you, Lord, for promising never to
turn your back on me. Amen.

Praise

I will declare your fame
      to all generations;
   therefore the nations will praise you
      for ever and ever.

Ps. 45:17, NEB

Proposal

All who are led by the Spirit of God are children of God.

Rom. 8:14, NRSV

Practice

Today I'll make every effort to be conscious of the Holy Spirit's presence and sensitive to the Spirit's leading.

Promise

We know that if the earthly tent we live in is destroyed, we have a building from God, an eternal house in heaven, not built by human hands.

2 Cor. 5:1, NIV

Prayer

Thank you, Lord, for the promise of a new body that will last forever. Amen.

Praise

Hannah also prayed and said,
"My heart exults in the Lord,
    my strength is exalted in the Lord. . . .
There is none holy like the Lord."

1 Sam. 2:1-2, RSV

Proposal

If we endure,
    we will also reign with [Christ].
If we disown him,
    he will also disown us.

2 Tim. 2:12, NIV

Practice

Today I'll be faithful to the Lord, to those
who depend upon me, and to those who
are new in the faith.

Promise

I will send you the Comforter—the Holy
Spirit, the source of all truth.

John 15:26, TLB

Prayer

Thank you, Lord, for the way the Holy Spirit
bonds me to you. What a privilege! Amen.

Praise

Let us give thanks to the God and Father of
our Lord Jesus Christ, the merciful Father,
the God from whom all help comes!

2 Cor. 1:3, TEV

Proposal

If we deliberately keep on sinning after we
have received the knowledge of the truth,
no sacrifice for sins is left.

Heb. 10:26, NIV

Practice

Today I'll do nothing to interrupt my fellowship with the Lord.

Promise

The Lord is the Spirit, and where the Spirit
of the Lord is, there is freedom.

2 Cor. 3:17, NIV

Prayer

Thank you, Lord, for delivering me from the
worst imprisonment of all—myself! Amen.

Praise

Thou art my God, and I will give thanks
    to thee;
  thou art my God, I will extol thee.

Ps. 118:28, RSV

Proposal

The reason you don't have what you want is
that you don't ask God for it.

Jas. 4:2, TLB

Practice

Today I'll make every effort to be in conscious contact with God. I'll praise God,
confess my sins, and pray for the needs of
others.

Promise

There shall be nothing in the city which is
evil; for the throne of God and of the Lamb
will be there, and his servants will worship
him.

Rev. 22:3, TLB

Prayer

Thank you, Lord, for the promise of a time
when evil will be no more. Amen.

February 18

Praise

I seemed to hear the great sound of a huge crowd in heaven, singing,

"Alleluia!

Victory and glory and power to our God!"

Rev. 19:1, JB

Proposal

If we say we are [God's] friends, but go on living in spiritual darkness and sin, we are lying.

1 John 1:6, TLB

Practice

Today I refuse to live with unforgiven sin. With the aid of the Holy Spirit, I'll review my life and ask God and others for forgiveness.

Promise

[Jesus said,] "Take my yoke upon you and learn from me, for I am gentle and humble . . . and you will find rest for your souls. For my yoke is easy and my burden is light."

Matt. 11:29-30, NIV

Prayer

Thank you, Lord, for the privilege of serving you and your glorious reign. Amen.

Praise

Let us come before his presence
    with thanksgiving,
and make a joyful noise unto him
    with psalms.

Ps. 95:2, KJV

Proposal

Whoever hates another believer is in the darkness, walks in the darkness, and does not know the way to go, because the darkness has brought on blindness.

1 John 2:11, NRSV

Practice

Today I refuse to harbor any thought of envy, jealousy, or anger.

Promise

Jesus Christ is the same yesterday and today and for ever.

Heb. 13:8, RSV

Prayer

Lord, you are the source of stability for my life. Material objects wear out, and people are fickle, but thank you, Lord, for always being true to your Word. Amen.

February 20

Praise

I will sing of your love and justice;
   to you, O Lord, I will sing praise.

Ps. 101:1, NIV

Proposal

If we say that we have no sin, we are only
fooling ourselves, and refusing to accept
the truth.

1 John 1:8, TLB

Practice

Today I'll take a personal inventory and
make a list of any sins and character defects.
Through Christ, I'll seek God's forgiveness
for the former and help for the latter.

Promise

Jesus looked at them and said, "For mortals
it is impossible, but for God all things are
possible."

Matt. 19:26, NRSV

Prayer

Thank you, Lord, for the hope that springs
eternal from your Word. Amen.

Praise

O come, let us worship and bow down:
    let us kneel before the Lord our maker.

Ps. 95:6, KJV

Proposal

Make every effort to supplement your faith
with virtue, and virtue with knowledge, and
knowledge with self-control, and self-
control with steadfastness.

2 Pet. 1:5-6, RSV

Practice

Today I'll be filled with the Holy Spirit and
focused on the fruit of self-control.

Promise

Every good and perfect gift is from above,
coming down from the Father of the
heavenly lights, who does not change like
shifting shadows.

Jas. 1:17, NIV

Prayer

Thank you, Lord, for spiritual blessings,
which are the source of joy. Amen.

Praise

He went with them into the temple courts, walking and jumping, and praising God.

Acts 3:8, NIV

Proposal

When you ask, you do not receive, because you seek with wrong motives, that you may spend what you get on your pleasures.

Jas. 4:3, NIV

Practice

Today I'll pray for needs that are in agreement with God's will.

Promise

Nothing impure will ever enter [the new Jerusalem], nor will anyone who does what is shameful or deceitful, but only those whose names are written in the Lamb's book of life.

Rev. 21:27, NIV

Prayer

Thank you, Lord, for the assurance that my name is written in the Lamb's book of life. Amen.

February 23

Praise

Bless the Lord, O you his angels,
   you mighty ones who do his word. . . .
Bless the Lord, all his hosts,
   his ministers that do his will!

Ps. 103:20-21, RSV

Proposal

If we say we have not sinned, we make
[God] a liar, and his word is not in us.

1 John 1:10, RSV

Practice

Today I'll examine my motives and ask the
Lord to forgive any unresolved sins.

Promise

Blessed are you when people revile you and
persecute you and utter all kinds of evil
against you falsely. . . . Rejoice and be glad,
for your reward is great in heaven.

Matt. 5:11-12, NRSV

Prayer

Thank you, Lord, for drawing me close to
you when I suffer for identifying with you
and your kingdom of righteousness. Amen.

Praise

Then the Levites . . . stood up and praised the Lord the God of Israel with a mighty shout.

2 Chron. 20:19, NEB

Proposal

If your heart turns away and you are not obedient . . . you will certainly be destroyed.

Deut. 30:17-18, NIV

Practice

Today I'll be obedient to the Lord by being sensitive to the leading of the Holy Spirit.

Promise

Our citizenship is in heaven. And we eagerly await a Savior from there, the Lord Jesus Christ, who . . . will transform our lowly bodies so that they will be like his glorious body.

Phil. 3:20-21, NIV

Prayer

Thank you, Lord, for our secure hope of glory and a place for us in heaven. Amen.

Praise

Raise your hands in prayer in the Temple,
and praise the Lord!

Ps. 134:2, TEV

Proposal

The Spirit of God came upon Azariah. . . .
He went out to meet Asa and said, . . . "The
Lord is with you when you are with him. If
you seek him, he will be found by you, but
if you forsake him, he will forsake you."

2 Chron. 15:1-2, NIV

Practice

Today I'll surrender to the Lord by forsaking
selfish ways.

Promise

To the one who conquers I will give a place
with me on my throne, just as I myself conquered and sat down with my Father on his
throne.

Rev. 3:21, NRSV

Prayer

Thank you, Lord, for the promise that one
day I will share your throne. Amen.

Praise

Enter his gates with thanksgiving
    and his courts with praise;
give thanks to him and praise his name.

Ps. 100:4, NIV

Proposal

Unless the Lord builds the house,
    its builders labor in vain.

Ps. 127:1, NIV

Practice

Today I'll spend time in meditation and
prayer before making a serious decision.

Promise

Jesus said to her, "Everyone who drinks of
this water will be thirsty again, but those
who drink of the water that I will give them
will never be thirsty. The water that I will
give will become in them a spring of water
gushing up to eternal life."

John 4:13-14, NRSV

Prayer

Thank you, Lord, for satisfying the deepest
longings of my soul. Amen.

Praise

Praise the Lord, my soul!
O Lord, my God, how great you are!
You are clothed with majesty and glory;
you cover yourself with light.

Ps. 104:1, TEV

Proposal

True praise is a worthy sacrifice; this really honors me. Those who walk my paths will receive salvation from the Lord.

Ps. 50:23, TLB

Practice

Today I'll praise the Lord with my lips, my thoughts, and my actions.

Promise

Blessed are those who mourn,
for they shall be comforted.

Matt. 5:4, RSV

Prayer

Thank you, Lord, for comforting me when the words and actions of others do not satisfy. Amen.

February 28

Praise

Oh, give thanks to the Lord, for he is good;
His love and his kindness go on forever.
Cry out to him, "Oh, save us, God of our
      salvation. . . .
Then we will thank your holy name,
And triumph in your praise."

1 Chron. 16:34-35, TLB

Proposal

If I had ignored my sins,
    the Lord would not have listened to me.

Ps. 66:18, TEV

Practice

Today I'll examine my life and deal with my
shortcomings as well as my sins.

Promise

When Christ who is your life is revealed,
then you also will be revealed with him in
glory.

Col. 3:4, NRSV

Prayer

Thank you, Lord, for the promise of sharing
your glory one day. Amen.

March 1

Praise

O God, thou art my God, I seek thee. . . .
Because thy steadfast love is better than life,
my lips will praise thee.

Ps. 63:1, 3, RSV

Proposal

Let each of you look not to your own interests, but to the interests of others.

Phil. 2:4, NRSV

Practice

Today I'll be sensitive to the needs of others
and alert for opportunities to help.

Promise

If you remain in me and my words remain
in you, ask whatever you wish, and it will be
given you.

John 15:7, NIV

Prayer

Thank you, Lord, for the Holy Spirit, who
illuminates Scripture and enables most pas-
sages to speak to me personally. Amen.

Praise

May those who delight in my vindication
   shout for joy and gladness;
may they always say, "The Lord be exalted,
   who delights in the well-being of
      his servant."

Ps. 35:27, NIV

Proposal

Pride only breeds quarrels,
   but wisdom is found in those who
   take advice.

Prov. 13:10, NIV

Practice

Today I'll yield to the guidance of the Holy
Spirit in all matters, important or not.

Promise

Ask, and you will be given what you ask for.
   Seek, and you will find.
   Knock, and the door will be opened.
For everyone who asks, receives.

Matt. 7:7-8, TLB

Prayer

Thank you, Lord, for never failing to answer
my prayers. Amen.

March 3

Praise

Hear this, you kings! Listen, you rulers!
　　I will sing to the Lord, I will sing;
I will make music to the Lord,
　　　the God of Israel.

Judg. 5:3, NIV

Proposal

I am the Lord your God, who brought you
out of . . . slavery. You shall have no other
gods before me.

Exod. 20:2-3, NIV

Practice

Today I'll renounce the idols and gods of
this world and worship solely God the
Father and my Lord and Savior Jesus Christ.

Promise

I shall put my spirit in you, and make you
keep my laws and sincerely respect my
observances.

Ezek. 36:27, JB

Prayer

Thank you, Lord, for consoling me and lifting my spirits when I suffer from low self-
esteem. Amen.

March 4

Praise

He gave them the lands of the nations . . .
that they might keep his precepts
  and observe his laws.
Praise the Lord.

Ps. 105:44-45, NIV

Proposal

The Lord does not see as mortals see; they
look on the outward appearance, but the
Lord looks on the heart.

1 Sam. 16:7, NRSV

Practice

Today I'll replace negative, disturbing
thoughts with secure, constructive ones
from memorized Scripture verses.

Promise

I no longer call you slaves, for a master
doesn't confide in his slaves; now you are
my friends.

John 15:15, TLB

Prayer

Thank you, Lord, for the glorious privilege
of being your friend. Amen.

Praise

Praise him, sun and moon;
   praise him, shining stars. . . .
Praise him, kings and all peoples,
   princes and all other rulers.

Ps. 148:3, 11, TEV

Proposal

In everything we do we show that we are
God's servants, by patiently enduring
trouble, hardships, and difficulties.

2 Cor. 6:4, TEV

Practice

Today I'll practice patience in all my affairs,
whether I am late, tired, or whatever.

Promise

[God] has made known to us . . . the
mystery of his will, according to his purpose
which he set forth in Christ . . . to unite all
things in [Christ].

Eph. 1:9-10, RSV

Prayer

Thank you, Lord, for revealing your will,
directing my life, and giving me hope.
Amen.

March 6

Praise

Blessed be the Lord God of Israel
    from everlasting to everlasting:
    and let all the people say, Amen.
Praise ye the Lord.

Ps. 106:48, KJV

Proposal

Learn to put aside your own desires so that
you will become patient and godly, gladly
letting God have his way with you

2 Pet. 1:6, TLB

Practice

Today I'll surrender my life to the Lord, so
that he may mold me into his image.

Promise

[The Lord] satisfies you with good
    as long as you live
so that your youth is renewed
    like the eagle's.

Ps. 103:5, NRSV

Prayer

Thank you, Lord, for who you are and the
blessings you bestow every day. Amen.

March 7

Praise

Praise the Lord, people of Israel;
   praise him, you priests of God!

Ps. 135:19, TEV

Proposal

We can rejoice . . . when we run into
problems and trials, for we know that they
are good for us—they help us learn to be
patient.

Rom. 5:3, TLB

Practice

Today I'll experience self-control, contentment, and the Lord's fellowship in every
situation.

Promise

I waited patiently for the Lord. . . .
He lifted me out of the slimy pit . . .
he set my feet on a rock
   and gave me a firm place to stand.

Ps. 40:1-2, NIV

Prayer

Thank you, Lord, for being the foundation
of my life. Amen.

March 8

Praise

Lift up your heads, O ye gates . . .
   and the King of glory shall come in.
Who is the King of glory?
The Lord of hosts, he is the King of glory.

Ps. 24:9-10, KJV

Proposal

Take heed lest you forget the Lord your
God, by not keeping his commandments,
. . . which I command you this day:

Deut. 8:11, RSV

Practice

Today I'll express my gratitude to the Lord
by obeying his commandments and doing
his will.

Promise

For our light and momentary troubles are
achieving for us an eternal glory that far out-
weighs them all.

2 Cor. 4:17, NIV

Prayer

Thank you, Lord, for always keeping your
promises and always answering prayer.
Amen.

March 9

Praise

Shout with joy to God, all the earth!
Sing the glory of his name;
offer him glory and praise!

Ps. 66:1-2, NIV

Proposal

When you give to the needy, do not let your
left hand know what your right hand is
doing, so that your giving may be in secret.

Matt. 6:3-4, NIV

Practice

Today I refuse to succumb to selfishness. I'll
give others my time and attention as
opportunities arise.

Promise

I tell you the truth, my Father will give you
whatever you ask in my name. . . . Ask and
you will receive, and your joy will be complete.

John 16:23-24, NIV

Prayer

Thank you, Lord, for being the source of my
strength. Amen.

March 10

Praise

Come, praise the Lord, all his servants,
  all who serve in his Temple at night.

Ps. 134:1, TEV

Proposal

You aren't made unholy by eating non-kosher food! It is what you say and think that makes you unclean.

Matt. 15:11, TLB

Practice

Today I'll say or do nothing that would bring dishonor to the Lord, my family, my fellow Christians, or myself.

Promise

My help comes from the Lord,
  who made heaven and earth. . . .
He who keeps you will not slumber. . . .
The Lord is your keeper.

Ps. 121:2-5, RSV

Prayer

Thank you, Lord, for being my protector day and night, day in and day out. Amen.

March 11

Praise

Let all those that put their trust in thee
    rejoice:
  let them ever shout for joy . . . :
let them also that love thy name
    be joyful in thee.

Ps. 5:11, KJV

Proposal

Each of you must give as you have made up
your mind, not reluctantly or under compul-
sion, for God loves a cheerful giver.

2 Cor. 9:7, NRSV

Practice

Today I'll gladly give to others because
giving is the key that opens the door to contentment.

Promise

I can do everything God asks me to with the
help of Christ who gives me the strength
and power.

Phil. 4:13, TLB

Prayer

Thank you, Lord, for the strength to complete my daily tasks. Amen.

Praise

I will praise you, O Lord, among the
      nations;
I will sing of you among the peoples.

Ps. 57:9, NIV

Proposal

To watch over mouth and tongue
    is to keep out of trouble.

Prov. 21:23, NRSV

Practice

Today I refuse to react negatively to the
shortcomings of others.

Promise

May our Lord Jesus Christ himself and God
our Father, who has loved us and given us
everlasting comfort and hope which we
don't deserve, comfort your hearts with all
comfort, and help you in every good thing
you say and do.

2 Thess. 2:16-17, TLB

Prayer

Thank you, Lord, for flooding my soul with
a peace that passes all understanding.
Amen.

Praise

Let everything that has breath
    praise the Lord.
Praise the Lord.

Ps. 150:6, NIV

Proposal

I tell you, do not worry about your life, what
you will eat or drink; or about your body,
what you will wear. Is not life more
important than food, and the body more
important than clothes?

Matt. 6:25, NIV

Practice

Today I'll experience life more fully by
refusing to take people, places, or things for
granted.

Promise

The Lord replied, "I myself will go with you
and give you success."

Exod. 33:14, TLB

Prayer

Thank you, Lord, for the times you have
definitely intervened on my behalf. Amen.

March 14

Praise

Praise [the Lord] with trumpet sound;
  praise him with lute and the harp!

Ps. 150:3, RSV

Proposal

Let us run with endurance the race that is
set before us, looking to Jesus, the author
and finisher of our faith.

Heb. 12:1-2, NKJB

Practice

Today I'll rise above problems by developing and maintaining an optimistic, positive
attitude toward people, places, and things.

Promise

[The Lord] gives power to the tired and
worn out, and strength to the weak.

Isa. 40:29, TLB

Prayer

Thank you, Lord, for managing my life and
affording me opportunities to achieve anything within my capabilities. Amen.

Praise

Let God's people rejoice in their triumph
  and sing joyfully all night long.
Let them shout aloud as they praise God.

Ps. 149:5-6, TEV

Proposal

Evil will not depart from the house
  of one who returns evil for good.

Prov. 17:13, NRSV

Practice

Today I'll ask the Lord to bless those who
cause me anguish by nit-picking or finding
fault.

Promise

If you believe, you will receive whatever
you ask for in prayer.

Matt. 21:22, TEV

Prayer

Thank you, Lord, for the faith to be
unafraid, to enjoy what is beautiful, to love,
and to believe that my loved ones also love
me. Amen.

Praise

Praise the Lord!
Israel's leaders bravely led;
The people gladly followed!
Yes, bless the Lord!

Judg. 5:2, TLB

Proposal

Submit yourselves . . . to God. Resist the
devil, and he will flee from you.

Jas. 4:7, NIV

Practice

Today I'll receive the power to resist Satan.
In every temptation I'll surrender to the
Lord and be filled with the Holy Spirit.

Promise

Give, and it will be given to you; good
measure, pressed down, shaken together,
running over, will be put into your lap.

Luke 6:38, RSV

Prayer

Thank you, Lord, for the numerous blessings that result from my giving, and from
giving by others. Amen.

Praise

I will indeed praise you with the harp;
    I will praise your faithfulness,
        my God.
On my harp I will play hymns to you,
    the Holy One of Israel.

Ps. 71:22, TEV

Proposal

Be patient . . . beloved, until the coming of
the Lord. The farmer waits for the precious
crop from the earth, being patient with it
until it receives the early and the late rains.
You also must be patient.

Jas. 5:7-8, NRSV

Practice

Today I'll practice patience by constantly
affirming the sovereignty of God.

Promise

For whoever finds me finds life
    and receives favor from the Lord.

Prov. 8:35, NIV

Prayer

Thank you, Lord, for the assurance that you
are always in control. Amen.

Praise

Be exalted, O God, above the heavens;
    let your glory be over all the earth.

Ps. 57:11, NIV

Proposal

Keep watch and pray that you will not fall
into temptation. The spirit is willing, but the
flesh is weak.

Matt. 26:41, TEV

Practice

Today I'll keep this book handy and use it
to keep tempting thoughts from lodging in
my imagination.

Promise

God is our shelter and strength,
    always ready to help in times of trouble.
So we will not be afraid, even if
        the earth is shaken
    and mountains fall into the ocean depths.

Ps. 46:1-2, TEV

Prayer

Thank you, Lord, for being my refuge in
times of trouble. Amen.

March 19

Praise

Praise [the Lord] with the clash of cymbals,
praise him with resounding cymbals.

Ps. 150:5, NIV

Proposal

Do not judge. . . . For in the same way you
judge others, you will be judged, and with
the measure you use, it will be measured
to you.

Matt. 7:1-2, NIV

Practice

Today I refuse to judge, speak ill, or be critical of anyone regardless of circumstances.

Promise

Wisdom and knowledge will be given you.
And I will also give you wealth, riches and
honor.

2 Chron. 1:12, NIV

Prayer

Thank you, Lord, for the Scriptures, whose
principles and instruction are a road map
for successful living. Amen.

March 20

Praise
You are enthroned as the Holy One;
    you are the praise of Israel.

Ps. 22:3, NIV

Proposal
Those who desire life
        and desire to see good days,
    let them keep their tongues from evil
        and their lips from speaking deceit.

1 Pet. 3:10, NRSV

Practice
Today I'll keep my tongue from evil by feeding my spirit with the Word of God, filling my soul with wholesome, holy thoughts, and surrendering my will to the Holy Spirit.

Promise
You will show me the path that leads to life;
    your presence fills me with joy
        and brings me pleasure for ever.

Ps. 16:11, TEV

Prayer
Thank you, Lord, for enriching my life immeasurably with your presence. Amen.

Praise

Ascribe to the Lord, O families of nations,
  ascribe to the Lord . . . the glory due
    his name. . . .
Worship the Lord in the splendor of
  his holiness.

1 Chron. 16:28-29, NIV

Proposal

Anyone who makes no mistakes in speaking is perfect, able to keep the whole body in check with a bridle.

Jas. 3:2, NRSV

Practice

If people do or say things today that irritate me, I refuse to react negatively with either words or actions.

Promise

The name of the Lord is a strong tower;
  the righteous run to it and are safe.

Prov. 18:10, NIV

Prayer

Thank you, Lord, for being a fortress that keeps me safe in the midst of evil. Amen.

Praise

Blessed be [God's] glorious name for ever:
    and let the whole earth be filled with
        his glory. Amen, and Amen.

Ps. 72:19, KJV

Proposal

Where there is no prophecy, the people
    cast off restraint,
    but happy are those who keep the law.

Prov. 29:18, NRSV

Practice

I'll approach this day as an adventure by
exploring new possibilities the Holy Spirit
will show me.

Promise

All who exalt themselves will be humbled,
and all who humble themselves will be
exalted.

Matt. 23:12, NRSV

Prayer

Thank you, Lord Jesus, for the lasting lesson
in humility you taught by your example in
washing the feet of your disciples. Amen.

Praise

All the earth bows down to you;
    they sing praise to you,
    they sing praise to your name.

Ps. 66:4, NIV

Proposal

Since . . . you have been raised with Christ,
set your hearts on things above, where
Christ is seated at the right hand of God.

Col. 3:1, NIV

Practice

Today I'll focus on trusting the Lord for happiness rather than depending on people,
places, or things.

Promise

Fear not, for I am with you,
    be not dismayed, for I am your God; . . .
I will uphold you with my victorious
    right hand.

Isa. 41:10, RSV

Prayer

Thank you, Lord, for your love which
purges me of fear. Amen.

Praise

I love the house where you live, O Lord,
    the place where your glory dwells. . . .
In the assembly of his people
    I praise the Lord.

Ps. 26:8, 12, TEV

Proposal

Observe the sabbath day, to keep it holy,
    as the Lord your God commanded you.

Deut. 5:12, RSV

Practice

To be restored, today I pledge to rest one
day a week. Next to worship, this will be
assigned highest priority.

Promise

Commit everything you do to the Lord.
    Trust him to help you do it and he will.

Ps. 37:5, TLB

Prayer

Thank you, Lord, for your trustworthiness
and dependability. Amen.

March 25

Praise

Sing praise to the Lord;
   tell the wonderful things he has done.

Ps. 105:2, TEV

Proposal

You understand that your faith is only put to the test to make you patient, but patience too is to have its practical results so that you will become fully-developed, complete, with nothing missing.

Jas. 1:3-4, JB

Practice

Today I'll practice patience by adhering to the principles of Scripture and by letting the Lord command my will.

Promise

God has not given us a spirit of fear, but of power and of love and of a sound mind.

2 Tim. 1:7, NKJB

Prayer

Thank you, Lord, for a sound mind and a healthy body. Amen.

Praise

Ascribe to the Lord the glory due his name;
worship the Lord
in the splendor of his holiness.

Ps. 29:2, NIV

Proposal

If any think they are religious, and do not
bridle their tongues but deceive their
hearts, their religion is worthless.

Jas. 1:26, NRSV

Practice

Today I'll make every effort to offend no
one by careless, insensitive, or derogatory
remarks.

Promise

Thus says the Lord, your Redeemer,
the Holy One of Israel;
"I am the Lord your God . . .
Who leads you in the way you should go."

Isa. 48:17, NASB

Prayer

Thank you, Lord, for showing me your will
each day. Amen.

Praise

Praise him with tambourine and dancing,
  praise him with the strings and flute.

Ps. 150:4, NIV

Proposal

Patience develops strength of character in
us and helps us trust God more each time
we use it until finally our hope and faith are
strong and steady.

Rom. 5:4, TLB

Practice

Today I'll practice patience by disciplining
my thoughts and considering the feelings of
others.

Promise

I will teach you what you are to do.

Exod. 4:15, NASB

Prayer

Thank you, Lord, for helping me know the
difference between the things I can change
and the things I cannot. Amen.

Praise

Glory in his holy name;
>let the hearts of those who seek the
>>Lord rejoice.

Look to the Lord and his strength;
>seek his face always.

Ps. 105:3-4, NIV

Proposal

You are God's man [or woman]. Run from all these evil things and work instead at what is right and good, learning to trust him and love others, and to be patient and gentle.

1 Tim. 6:11, TLB

Practice

Today I'll focus on trusting God by practicing the counsel of the Bible in all my affairs.

Promise

You have come to fullness in [Christ], who is the head of every ruler and authority.

Col. 2:10, NRSV

Prayer

Thank you, Lord, for being the chief provider of all my needs. Amen.

Praise

Save us, O Lord our God,
    and gather us from among the heathen,
to give thanks unto thy holy name,
    and to triumph in thy praise.

Ps. 106:47, KJV

Proposal

We do not want any of you to grow slack,
but to follow the example of those who
through sheer patient faith came to possess
the promises.

Heb. 6:12, Phillips

Practice

Today I'll make a gratitude list and take
nothing or no one for granted.

Promise

We are able to hold our heads high no matter what happens . . . [because] God loves
us and . . . has given us the Holy Spirit to fill
our hearts with his love.

Rom. 5:5, TLB

Prayer

Thank you, Lord, for filling my heart with
love. Amen.

March 30

Praise

My heart is with the commanders of Israel,
with the people who gladly volunteered.
Praise the Lord!

Judg. 5:9, TEV

Proposal

Stay always within the boundaries where
God's love can reach and bless you. Wait
patiently for the eternal life that our Lord
Jesus Christ in his mercy is going to give
you.

Jude 21, TLB

Practice

Today I'll open myself to God's grace
through prayer, meditation, Scripture, and
Christian fellowship.

Promise

If you ask me for anything in my name,
I will do it.

John 14:14, TEV

Prayer

Thank you, Lord, for answering my prayers
even though many times the answer is *no,*
or *not now.* Amen.

Praise

Praise the Lord, the God of Israel!
   He alone does these wonderful things.
Ps. 72:18, TEV

Proposal

Always obey the Lord
   and you will be happy.
If you are stubborn,
   you will be ruined.
Prov. 28:14, TEV

Practice

If tragedy strikes today, I refuse to blame
God or press him for answers when there
are none. My response will always be one
of thanksgiving.

Promise

If you have faith as small as a mustard seed,
you can say to this mountain, "Move from
here to there" and it will move.
Matt. 17:20, NIV

Prayer

Thank you, Lord, for the power to change
things through prayer. Amen.

April 1

Praise

All Israel brought up the ark of the covenant of the Lord with shouts, with the sounding of rams' horns and trumpets, and of cymbals, and playing of lyres and harps.

1 Chron. 15:28, NIV

Proposal

The more you talk,
   the more likely you are to sin.
If you are wise,
   you will keep quiet.

Prov. 10:19, TEV

Practice

Today I'll discipline my thoughts and condition myself to act rather than react.

Promise

Call upon Me [the Lord]
   in the day of trouble;
I shall rescue you,
   and you will honor Me.

Ps. 50:15, NASB

Prayer

Thank you, Lord, for help in times of trouble. Amen.

April 2

Praise

I cried out to him with my mouth;
    his praise was on my tongue....
Praise be to God,
    who has not rejected my prayer
    or withheld his love from me!

Ps. 66:17, 20, NIV

Proposal

We must never get tired of doing good
because if we don't give up the struggle we
shall get our harvest at the proper time.

Gal. 6:9, JB

Practice

Today I'll find pleasure in helping others
because of my love for the Lord Jesus
Christ.

Promise

Faith in Jesus' name—faith given us from
God—has caused this perfect healing.

Acts 3:16, TLB

Prayer

Thank you, Lord, for making me whole in
spirit, mind, and body. Amen.

April 3

Praise

Sing for joy to God our strength;
    shout aloud to the God of Jacob!
Begin the music, strike the tambourine,
    play the melodious harp and lyre.

Ps. 81:1-2, NIV

Proposal

Let us hold on firmly to the hope we
profess, because we can trust God to keep
his promise.

Heb. 10:23, TEV

Practice

Today I'll allow nothing to hinder my
resolve to praise God in all things.

Promise

To be controlled by human nature results in
death; to be controlled by the Spirit results
in life and peace.

Rom. 8:6, TEV

Prayer

Thank you, Lord, for the gift of salvation,
which makes abundant living possible.
Amen.

Praise

Let us rejoice and exult and give him
the glory,
for the marriage of the Lamb has come,
and his Bride has made herself ready.

Rev. 19:7, RSV

Proposal

If you will obey me, [the Lord,] and keep my
covenant, you will be my own people. The
whole earth is mine, but you will be my
chosen people.

Exod. 19:5, TEV

Practice

Today I'll show compassion and a willingness to listen to anyone who needs to
unload some burdens.

Promise

The Lord gives strength to his people;
the Lord blesses his people with peace.

Ps. 29:11, NIV

Prayer

Thank you, Lord, for the peace I experience
every day. Amen.

Praise

Who shall not fear thee, O Lord,
   and glorify thy name?
for thou only art holy:
for all nations shall come
   and worship before thee.

Rev. 15:4, KJV

Proposal

The Lord hates . . . a lying tongue.

Prov. 6:16 17, RSV

Practice

Today I'll be straightforward and honest
with myself as well as with everyone I meet.

Promise

[Jesus] was crucified in weakness, yet he
lives by God's power. Likewise, we are
weak in him, yet by God's power we will
live with him.

2 Cor. 13:4, NIV

Prayer

Thank you, Lord, for my earnest desire to
worship and praise you. Amen.

Praise

I praise you, Lord, because you heard me,
   because you have given me victory.

Ps. 118:21, TEV

Proposal

I will pray morning, noon, and night, pleading aloud with God; and he will hear and answer.

Ps. 55:17, TLB

Practice

Today I'll meditate on God's Word and the new insights the Holy Spirit will show me.

Promise

[Jesus] healed all who were sick. This was to fulfil what was spoken by the prophet Isaiah, "He took our infirmities and bore our diseases."

Matt. 8:16-17, RSV

Prayer

Thank you, Lord, for healing old wounds so that they no longer rise up and cause me problems. Amen.

April 7

Praise

O give thanks to the Lord, for he is good;
  for his steadfast love endures for ever!

Ps. 107:1, RSV

Proposal

You shall keep [the Lord's] statutes and his
commandments, which I command you
this day, that it may go well with you, and
with your children after you.

Deut. 4:40, RSV

Practice

Today I'll live by the authority of Scripture
in every situation.

Promise

The fruit of the Spirit is love, joy, peace,
patience, kindness, generosity, faithfulness,
gentleness, and self-control. There is no law
against such things.

Gal. 5:22, NRSV

Prayer

Thank you, Lord, for the fruit which the
Holy Spirit produces in my life. Amen.

Praise

Let the peoples praise thee, O God;
    let all the peoples praise thee!

Ps. 67:3, RSV

Proposal

Praise the Lord!
Happy are those who fear the Lord,
    who greatly delight in his
        commandments.

Ps. 112:1, NRSV

Practice

Today I'll approach the Lord with thanksgiving in my heart and praise on my lips.

Promise

[God] is able to keep you from slipping and falling away, and to bring you, sinless and perfect, into his glorious presence with mighty shouts of everlasting joy.

Jude 24-25, TLB

Prayer

Thank you, Lord, for revealing yourself to me and keeping me from falling. Amen.

Praise

The waters swallowed their oppressors,
    not one of them was left.
Then, having faith in his promises,
    they immediately sang his praises.

Ps. 106:11-12, JB

Proposal

I beg you to obey the Lord's message; then
all will go well with you, and your life will be
spared.

Jer. 38:20, TEV

Practice

Today I'll surrender my life to Jesus and
point others toward him as the Spirit leads.

Promise

God is always at work in you to make you
willing and able to obey his own purpose.

Phil. 2:13, TEV

Prayer

Thank you, Lord, for intuitive thoughts and
insights that enable me to grow spiritually
and understand myself more fully. Amen.

April 10

Praise

Glory in his holy name;
> let the hearts of those who seek the Lord
> rejoice.

1 Chron. 16:10, NIV

Proposal

Let heaven fill your thoughts; don't spend
your time worrying about things down
here. . . . Your real life is in heaven with
Christ and God.

Col. 3:2-3, TLB

Practice

Today I'll accept life on life's terms by relying on the Holy Spirit to supply secure
thoughts regardless of circumstances.

Promise

When I am surrounded by troubles,
> you, [O Lord,] keep me safe.
You oppose my angry enemies
> and save me by your power.

Ps. 138:7, TEV

Prayer

Thank you, Lord, for your promises, which
serve as a stronghold for my life. Amen.

April 11

Praise

I will put my hope in God,
    and once again I will praise him,
        my savior and my God.

Ps. 43:5, TEV

Proposal

All who obey [God's] commandments abide
in him, and he abides in them. And by this
we know that he abides in us, by the Spirit
that he has given us

1 John 3:24, NRSV

Practice

Today I refuse to rationalize my way out of
doing the Lord's will.

Promise

Because the Lord is my Shepherd, I have
everything I need!

Ps. 23:1, TLB

Prayer

Thank you, Lord, for revealing my
innermost needs and satisfying the desires
of my heart. Amen.

April 12

Praise

My soul will boast in the Lord;
    let the afflicted hear and rejoice.
Glorify the Lord with me;
    let us exalt his name together.

Ps. 34:2-3, NIV

Proposal

If my people . . . will humble themselves
and pray and seek my face and turn from
their wicked ways, then will I hear . . .
forgive their sin, and . . . heal their land.

2 Chron. 7:14, NIV

Practice

Today I'll pray for political leaders
throughout the world.

Promise

You will also be a crown of beauty
    in the hand of the Lord,
And a royal diadem
    in the hand of your God.

Isa. 62:3, NASB

Prayer

Thank you, Lord, for molding me into
a vessel you can use. Amen.

April 13

Praise

At midnight Paul and Silas prayed, and sang praises unto God: and the prisoners heard them.

Acts 16:25, KJV

Proposal

Don't you know that friendship with the world is hatred toward God? Anyone who chooses to be a friend of the world becomes an enemy of God.

Jas. 4:4, NIV

Practice

Today my actions will be directed by the Holy Spirit rather than by feelings, impulses, sensations, or circumstances.

Promise

My God will meet all your needs according to his glorious riches in Christ Jesus.

Phil. 4:19, NIV

Prayer

Thank you, Lord, for being ready to meet any emergency. Amen.

Praise

Praise our God, O peoples,
  let the sound of his praise be heard.

Ps. 66:8, NIV

Proposal

Do your best to present yourself to God as one approved by him, a worker who has no need to be ashamed, rightly explaining the word of truth.

2 Tim. 2:15, NRSV

Practice

By wisely planning and using my time today, I'll bolster my self-esteem, spiritual development, and sense of well-being.

Promise

"I will restore you to health
  And I will heal you of your wounds,"
    declares the Lord.

Jer. 30:17, NASB

Prayer

Thank you, Lord, for my healthy body, soul, and spirit. Amen.

Praise

For God is the King of all the earth;
     sing ye praises with understanding.

Ps. 47:7, KJV

Proposal

The whole Bible was given to us by inspiration from God and is useful to teach us what is true and to make us realize what is wrong in our lives; it straightens us out and helps us do what is right.

2 Tim. 3:16, TLB

Practice

Today I'll focus on Scripture to transform me as well as to inform me.

Promise

[The Lord] satisfies the thirsty
     and fills the hungry with good things.

Ps. 107:9, NIV

Prayer

Thank you, Lord, for the contentment that comes from living by your purpose, not by my own selfish schemes. Amen.

April 16

Praise

And the twenty-four elders and the four
living creatures fell down and worshiped
God who is seated on the throne, saying,
   "Amen, Hallelujah!"

Rev. 19:4, RSV

Proposal

The Lord is faithful to his promises. Blessed
are all those who wait for him to help them.

Isa. 30:18, TLB

Practice

Today I'll spend time with the Lord and
consult with others before making
important decisions.

Promise

The Lord . . . protects the lives of his people;
   he rescues them from the
      power of the wicked.

Ps. 97:10, TEV

Prayer

Thank you, Lord, for a peaceful mind which
affords me restful sleep and clear thinking.
Amen.

Praise

I, with a song of thanksgiving,
 will sacrifice to you.
What I have vowed I will make good.
 Salvation comes from the Lord.

Jon. 2:9, NIV

Proposal

Your words are what sustain me; they are
food to my hungry soul. They bring joy to
my sorrowing heart and delight me.

Jer. 15:16, TLB

Practice

Today I'll receive inspiration and
encouragement from cheerful thoughts and
a grateful attitude.

Promise

The young lions do lack and suffer hunger;
But they who seek the Lord
 shall not be in want of any good thing.

Ps. 34:10, NASB

Prayer

Thank you, Lord, for a clean conscience.
Amen.

April 18

Praise

I will praise the Lord
   no matter what happens.
I will constantly speak of
   his glories and grace.

Ps. 34:1, TLB

Proposal

Whatever you do, whether in word or deed,
do it all in the name of the Lord Jesus,
giving thanks to God the Father through
him.

Col. 3:17, NIV

Practice

Today I'll obey the Lord in spite of difficult
circumstances, dull feelings, or distractions.

Promise

[Jesus] personally bore our sins in his own
body on the cross, so that we might be dead
to sin and be alive to all that is good.

1 Pet. 2:24, Phillips

Prayer

Thank you, Lord, for suffering on my behalf
and for healing me. Amen.

April 19

Praise

Four thousand are to praise the Lord with the musical instruments . . . to stand every morning to thank and praise the Lord . . . to do the same in the evening.

1 Chron. 23:5, 30, NIV

Proposal

Dirty stories, foul talk and coarse jokes—these are not for you. Instead, remind each other of God's goodness and be thankful.

Eph. 5:4, TLB

Practice

Today I'll guard my speech against grieving the Holy Spirit.

Promise

As a mother comforts her child,
    so will I comfort you.

Isa. 66:13, NIV

Prayer

Thank you, Lord, for comforting me when I have trouble accepting something I cannot change. Amen.

Praise

Praise the Lord from the earth, . . .
    and all ocean depths: . . .
    strong winds that obey his command.

Ps. 148:7-8, TEV

Proposal

How happy are those who hear the word of
God and obey it!

Luke 11:28, TEV

Practice

Today I'll accept the Bible as the inspired
Word of God and obey God's word to me.

Promise

[God] did not hesitate to spare his own Son
but gave him up for us all—can we not trust
such a God to give us, with him, everything
else that we can need?

Rom. 8:32, Phillips

Prayer

Thank you, Lord, for your precious Spirit,
who enables me to overcome fear, control
my temper, and love the unlovable. Amen.

April 21

Praise

Then our mouth was filled with laughter,
    and our tongue with shouts of joy;
then it was said among the nations,
    "The Lord has done great things for them."

Ps. 126:2, NRSV

Proposal

Your word is a lamp to my feet
    and a light for my path.

Ps. 119:105, NIV

Practice

Today I'll meditate on the Sermon on the
Mount and practice its teachings in my deal-
ings with others: Matthew 5—7.

Promise

I have been young, and now am old,
    yet I have not seen the righteous
        forsaken
    or their children begging bread.

Ps. 37:25, NRSV

Prayer

Thank you, Lord, for being patient with me
when I'm stubborn and preoccupied with
myself. Amen.

April 22

Praise

Everyone will praise his great
    and majestic name.
  Holy is he!

Ps. 99:3, TEV

Proposal

The prayer of faith will save the sick, and
the Lord will raise them up; and anyone
who has committed sins will be forgiven.

Jas. 5:15, NRSV

Practice

Today I'll make a list of every sick person
who comes to mind and pray for each one
individually.

Promise

But [the Lord] said to me,
    "My grace is sufficient for you, for
    my power is made perfect in weakness."

2 Cor. 12:9, RSV

Prayer

Thank you, Lord, for enabling me to see life
as a journey rather than a destination.
Amen.

April 23

Praise

[David] appointed some of the Levites . . .
to make petition, to give thanks, and to
praise the Lord, the God of Israel.

1 Chron. 16:4, NIV

Proposal

The Lord your God is the faithful God who
for a thousand generations keeps his
promises and constantly loves those who
love him and who obey his commands.

Deut. 7:9, TLB

Practice

Today I'll experience contentment by
adhering to the promises of Psalm 23.

Promise

I, [Jesus,] am leaving you with a gift—peace
of mind and heart! And the peace I give
isn't fragile. . . . So don't be troubled
or afraid.

John 14:27, TLB

Prayer

Thank you, Lord, for every resource I need
to live free of anxiety and fear. Amen.

Praise

Sing to [the Lord], sing praise to him;
 tell of all his wonderful acts.

1 Chron. 16:9, NIV

Proposal

Let your roots grow down into [Christ] and draw up nourishment from him. See that you go on growing in the Lord, and become strong and vigorous in the truth you were taught. Let your lives overflow with joy and thanksgiving for all he has done.

Col. 2:7, TLB

Practice

Today I'll praise the Lord *in* all things but not necessarily *for* all things.

Promise

[God] does not forget the cry
 of the afflicted.

Ps. 9:12, NRSV

Prayer

Thank you, Lord, for always coming through when I need you. Amen.

April 25

Praise

Let the nations praise you, God,
   let all the nations praise you!

Ps. 67:5, JB

Proposal

Obey my voice, and I will be your God, and
you will be My people; and you will walk in
all the way which I command you, that it
may be well with you.

Jer. 7:23, NASB

Practice

Today I'll serve the Lord by opening myself
to the Holy Spirit and by helping others.

Promise

Great peace have they who love your law,
      [O Lord,]
   and nothing can make them stumble.

Ps. 119:165, NIV

Prayer

Thank you, Lord, for loving me when I'm
tired and grouchy and extremely unlovable.
Amen.

April 26

Praise

Sing praises to God, sing praises;
    sing praises unto our King, sing praises.

Ps. 47:6, KJV

Proposal

Repent and be baptized, every one of you,
in the name of Jesus Christ so that your sins
may be forgiven. And you will receive the
gift of the Holy Spirit.

Acts 2:38, NIV

Practice

Today I'll confess my sins, think merciful
thoughts, and pray for those who cause me
anguish.

Promise

The blessing of the Lord brings wealth,
    and he adds no trouble to it.

Prov. 10:22, NIV

Prayer

Thank you, Lord, for your inner presence
which enables me to handle any situation.
Amen.

April 27

Praise
Sing and make music in your heart to the Lord, always giving thanks to God the Father for everything, in the name of our Lord Jesus Christ.

Eph. 5:19-20, NIV

Proposal
Let your gentleness be evident to all. The Lord is near.

Phil. 4:5, NIV

Practice
Today I'll experience self-control by refusing to let my moods master me.

Promise
[The Lord] protects you day and night. He keeps you from all evil, and preserves your life. He keeps his eye upon you as you come and go, and always guards you.

Ps. 121:6-8, TLB

Prayer
Thank you, Lord, for showing me that inner security is found in you, not in people, places, or things. Amen.

April 28

Praise

Then I heard what seemed to be the voice of a great multitude, like the sound of many waters, . . . crying, "Hallelujah! For the Lord our God the Almighty reigns."

Rev. 19:6, RSV

Proposal

Don't you know that your body is the temple of the Holy Spirit, who lives in you?

1 Cor. 6:19, TEV

Practice

Today I'll minister to my temple of the Holy Spirit with nourishing fuel, stimulating exercise, and periods of quality rest.

Promise

I am sure that God . . . will keep right on helping you grow in his grace until . . . that day when Jesus Christ returns.

Phil. 1:6, TLB

Prayer

Thank you, Lord, for the healthy feeling I always enjoy after a good physical workout. Amen.

April 29

Praise

Praise the Lord with the harp;
    make music to him on the
        ten-stringed lyre.
Sing to him a new song;
    play skillfully, and shout for joy.

Ps. 33:2-3, NIV

Proposal

"You will seek me and find me when you
seek me with all your heart. I will be found
by you," declares the Lord.

Jer. 29:13-14, NIV

Practice

Today I'll be receptive toward opportunities
to minister in Jesus' name.

Promise

For you who fear my name
    the sun of righteousness shall rise,
        with healing in its wings.

Mal. 4:2, RSV

Prayer

Thank you, Lord, for healing me spiritually
and making me whole. Amen.

April 30

Praise

Tremble before him, all the earth! . . .
Let the heavens rejoice,
     let the earth be glad;
   let them say among the nations,
     "The Lord reigns!"

1 Chron. 16:30-31, NIV

Proposal

Don't use bad language. Say only what is
good and helpful to those you are talking to,
and what will give them a blessing.

Eph. 4:29, TLB

Practice

Today I'll use words to encourage others in
the way of righteousness and blessing.

Promise

The salvation of the righteous is
     from the Lord;
   he is their refuge in the time of trouble.
The Lord helps them and rescues them.

Ps. 37:39-40, NRSV

Prayer

Thank you, Lord, for coming to my aid
when I make a mess of things. Amen.

Praise

I will praise you as long as I live,
    and in your name I will lift up my hands.

Ps. 63:4, NIV

Proposal

You should be clothed in sincere compassion, in kindness and humility, gentleness and patience. Bear with one another; forgive each other as soon as a quarrel begins.

Col. 3:12-13, JB

Practice

Today I'll treat everyone with compassion and kindness, regardless of how they treat me.

Promise

I will be your God through all your lifetime, yes, even when your hair is white with age.

Isa. 46:4, TLB

Prayer

Thank you, Lord, for the assurance that you will never leave me, in this life or the next. Amen.

Praise

In that day you will say:
"Give thanks to the Lord, call on his name;
    make known among the nations
        what he has done,
    and proclaim that his name is exalted."

Isa. 12:4, NIV

Proposal

One does not live by bread alone,
    but by every word that comes
        from the mouth of God.

Matt. 4:4, NRSV

Practice

If disturbing thoughts come to mind today,
I'll replace them with promises from the
Word of God.

Promise

If two of you agree on earth about anything
they ask, it will be done for them by my
Father in heaven.

Matt. 18:19, RSV

Prayer

Thank you, Lord, for the power that results
from agreeing with others in prayer. Amen.

Praise

The circumcised believers . . . were astounded that the gift of the Holy Spirit had been poured out even on the Gentiles, for they heard them speaking in tongues and extolling God.

Acts 10:45-47, NRSV

Proposal

Above all, love each other deeply, because love covers over a multitude of sins.

1 Pet. 4:8, NIV

Practice

Today I'll seek opportunities to serve others in Jesus' name.

Promise

In this man Jesus, there is forgiveness for your sins! Everyone who trusts in him is freed from all guilt and declared righteous.

Acts 13:38-39, TLB

Prayer

Thank you, Lord, for cleansing my soul and spirit and freeing me from guilt. Amen.

Praise

How wonderful are the things
    the Lord does! . . .
He is to be praised forever.

Ps. 111:2, 10, TEV

Proposal

Take care, brothers and sisters, that none of
you . . . turns away from the living God. But
exhort one another . . . so that none of you
may be hardened by the deceitfulness of
sin.

Heb. 3:12-13, NRSV

Practice

If I stumble and fall into sin today, I'll
immediately seek the Lord's forgiveness.

Promise

When I lie down, I go to sleep in peace;
    you alone, O Lord, keep me perfectly safe.

Ps. 4:8, TEV

Prayer

Thank you, Lord, for the inner security and
calm assurance your presence gives me.
Amen.

May 5

Praise

Praise him—he is your God, and you have
seen with your own eyes the great and
astounding things that he has done for you.

Deut. 10:21, TEV

Proposal

Be patient with everyone. Make sure that
nobody pays back wrong for wrong, but
always try to be kind to each other and to
everyone else.

1 Thess. 5.14-15, NIV

Practice

Today I'll practice tolerance by remembering that when people do things that irritate
me, their purpose is not to irritate me.

Promise

As far as the east is from the west,
   So far has He removed our
      transgressions from us.

Ps. 103:12, NASB

Prayer

Thank you, Lord, for the inner joy that
results from knowing you loved me enough
to die for me. Amen.

Praise

In that day you will say:
"I will praise you, O Lord.
   Although you were angry with me,
your anger has turned away
   and you have comforted me."

Isa. 12:1, NIV

Proposal

Offer yourselves as a living sacrifice to God,
dedicated to his service and pleasing to
him. This is the true worship that you
should offer.

Rom. 12:1, TEV

Practice

Today I'll serve the Lord by being obedient
and seeking to please God rather than self.

Promise

I am the God who forgives your sins,
   and I do this because of who I am.
I will not hold your sins against you.

Isa. 43:25, TEV

Prayer

Thank you, Lord, for being willing to forgive
me as I forgive others. Amen.

Praise

Let them praise his name in the dance:
> let them sing praises unto him
>> with the timbrel and harp.

Ps. 149:3, KJV

Proposal

Don't repay evil for evil. Don't snap back at those who say unkind things about you. Instead, pray for God's help for them, for we are to be kind to others, and God will bless us for it.

1 Pet. 3:9, TLB

Practice

Today I'll show concern and kindness toward everyone I meet.

Promise

Though my father and my mother forsake
> me,
>> the Lord will take me into his care.

Ps. 27:10, NEB

Prayer

Thank you, Lord, for caring for me even if my parents abandon me through their choice or through death. Amen.

Praise

Now, our God, we give you thanks,
and praise your glorious name.

1 Chron. 29:13, NIV

Proposal

Put away from you all bitterness and wrath
and anger and wrangling and slander,
together with all malice.

Eph. 4:31, NRSV

Practice

Today I'll ferret out and dismiss bitterness
toward anyone, living or dead.

Promise

The righteous will flourish like a palm tree,
they will grow like a cedar of Lebanon;
planted in the house of the Lord,
they will flourish in the courts of our God.
They will still bear fruit in old age,
they will stay fresh and green.

Ps. 92:12-14, NIV

Prayer

Thank you, Lord, for helping me remain
young at heart despite an aging body.
Amen.

Praise

May my prayer be set before you
>like incense;
>>may the lifting up of my hands be
>>like the evening sacrifice.

Ps. 141:2, NIV

Proposal

My child, do not regard lightly the discipline
of the Lord, or lose heart when you are
punished by him; for the Lord disciplines
those whom he loves, and chastises every
child whom he accepts.

Heb. 12:5-6, NRSV

Practice

Today I refuse to entertain fearful thoughts
or become discouraged.

Promise

When tempted, no one should say, "God is
tempting me." For God cannot be tempted
by evil, nor does he tempt anyone.

Jas. 1:13, NIV

Prayer

Thank you, Lord, for enabling me to resist
temptation. Amen.

Praise

Praise the Lord, you Levites;
  praise him, all you that worship him.

Ps. 135:20, TEV

Proposal

Don't allow yourself to be overpowered
with evil. Take the offensive—overpower
evil by good!

Rom. 12:21, Phillips

Practice

Today I'll pray for people who do not act
justly toward me.

Promise

[God] saved us, not because of any works of
righteousness that we had done, but
according to his mercy, through the water
of rebirth and renewal by the Holy Spirit.
This Spirit he poured out on us richly
through Jesus Christ our Savior.

Titus 3:5-6, NRSV

Prayer

Thank you, Lord, for the Holy Spirit who
enables me to focus on God my Savior and
Jesus my Savior. Amen.

Praise

Write down for the coming generation
     what the Lord has done,
     so that people not yet born will
          praise him.

Ps. 102:18, TEV

Proposal

Dear friends, never avenge yourselves.
Leave that to God, for he has said that he
will repay those who deserve it.

Rom. 12:19, TLB

Practice

Today I'll deal creatively with anger by looking for humor in every situation.

Promise

God keeps his promise, and he will not
allow you to be tested beyond your power
to remain firm . . . he will give you the
strength to endure it, and so provide you
with a way out.

1 Cor. 10:13, TEV

Prayer

Thank you, Lord, for your grace, which is
sufficient in all circumstances. Amen.

Praise

Sing unto the Lord a new song,
 and his praise from the end of the earth,
ye that go down to the sea,
 and all that is therein;
 and the inhabitants thereof.

Isa. 42:10, KJV

Proposal

I don't want your sacrifices—I want your
love; I don't want your offerings—I want
you to know me.

Hos. 6:6, TLB

Practice

Today I'll enjoy a confident attitude by
focusing on God's promises.

Promise

In order to set us free from this present evil
age, Christ gave himself for our sins, in
obedience to the will of our God and
Father.

Gal. 1:4, TEV

Prayer

Thank you, Lord, for freeing me from the
bondage of sin. Amen.

Praise

I will praise thee;
    for I am fearfully and wonderfully made:
marvelous are thy works.

Ps. 139:14, KJV

Proposal

All of you, have unity of spirit, sympathy,
love for one another, a tender heart, and a
humble mind.

1 Pet. 3:8, NRSV

Practice

If I become irritated by the shortcomings of
others today, I'll remember my own failings.

Promise

Once again you will have compassion on
us. You will tread our sins beneath your
feet; you will throw them into the depths of
the ocean!

Mic. 7:19, TLB

Prayer

Thank you, Lord, for being patient with me
when I stumble and fall. Amen.

May 14

Praise

The Lord is my rock, my fortress and
      my deliverer. . . .
He is my stronghold, my refuge and
      my savior. . . .
I call to the Lord, who is worthy of praise.

2 Sam. 22:2-4, NIV

Proposal

Yet even now, says the Lord,
    return to me with all your heart,
with fasting, with weeping,
    and with mourning;
    rend your hearts and not your clothing.

Joel 2:12-13, NRSV

Practice

Today I'll depend upon the Lord and trust
him without reservation.

Promise

Overwhelming victory is ours through
Christ who loved us enough to die for us.

Rom. 8:37, TLB

Prayer

Thank you, Lord, for the contentment I
enjoy when spending time with you. Amen.

May 15

Praise

Surely God is my salvation. . . .
The Lord, the Lord is my strength
   and my song;
   he has become my salvation.

Isa. 12:2, NIV

Proposal

God's correction is always right and for our best good, that we may share his holiness. Being punished isn't enjoyable while it is happening—it hurts! But afterwards we can see the result, a quiet growth in grace and character.

Heb. 12:10-11, TLB

Practice

Today I'll look for good in every situation, even in failure.

Promise

[The Lord] grants sleep to those he loves.

Ps. 127:2, NIV

Prayer

Thank you, Lord, for the secure thoughts I enjoy by placing my life in your hands. Amen.

May 16

Praise
At midnight I rise to praise you,
    because of your righteous ordinances.
Ps. 119:62, NRSV

Proposal
[Jesus said,] "If you love me, you will keep
my commandments."
John 14:15, RSV

Practice
Today I'll meditate on the commandments
of Jesus and rely on the Holy Spirit for
guidance.

Promise
This is the assurance we have in approach-
ing God: that if we ask anything according
to his will, he hears us. And if we know that
he hears—whatever we ask—we know that
we have what we asked of him.
1 John 5:14-15, NIV

Prayer
Thank you, Lord, for the faith to believe that
my needs will always be satisfied. Amen.

Praise

O God, thy way is holy;
what god is so great as our God . . .
   who [works] miracles?

Ps. 77:13-14, NEB

Proposal

My command is this: Love each other as I
have loved you.

John 15:12, NIV

Practice

Today I'll show kindness to others and
stand ready to lend an ear to anyone who
needs it.

Promise

My sheep hear my voice, and I know them,
and they follow me; and I give them eternal
life, and they shall never perish, and no one
shall snatch them out of my hand.

John 10:27-28, RSV

Prayer

Thank you, Lord, for the assurance that
nothing can separate your love from me.
Amen.

May 18

Praise

How I long for your saving help,
   O Lord! . . .
Give me life, so that I may praise you.

Ps. 119:174-175, TEV

Proposal

What does the Lord your God ask of you but
to fear the Lord your God, to walk in all his
ways, to love him, to serve [him] . . . and to
observe the Lord's commands and decrees?

Deut. 10:12-13, NIV

Practice

Today I'll set goals and work toward them
with guidance and power from God's Spirit.

Promise

Happy are those whose help is . . . God, . . .
who made heaven and earth,
   the sea and all that is in them;
who keeps faith forever,
   who executes justice for the oppressed.

Ps. 146:5-7, NRSV

Prayer

Thank you, Lord, for always fulfilling your
promises. Amen.

May 19

Praise

The heavens praise your wonders, O Lord,
   your faithfulness too, in the assembly
      of the holy ones.

Ps. 89:5, NIV

Proposal

I urge you to live a life worthy of the calling
you have received. Be completely humble
and gentle; be patient, bearing with one
another in love.

Eph. 4:1-2, NIV

Practice

Today I'll see selfish pride and arrogance
for what they are—spiritual diseases that
war upon the soul.

Promise

Our earthly bodies . . . must be transformed
into heavenly bodies that cannot perish but
will live forever.

1 Cor. 15:53, TLB

Prayer

Thank you, Lord, for the imperishable body
I'll receive one day. Amen.

Praise

The priests took their positions, as did the
Levites with the Lord's musical instruments,
which King David had made for praising
the Lord . . . "His love endures forever."

2 Chron. 7:6, NIV

Proposal

Be kind to each other, tenderhearted,
forgiving one another, just as God has
forgiven you because you belong to Christ.

Eph. 4:32, TLB

Practice

Today I'll be kind to others, regardless of
my mood or predisposition.

Promise

He has put his brand upon us . . . and given
us his Holy Spirit . . . as the first installment
of all that he is going to give us.

2 Cor. 1:22, TLB

Prayer

Thank you, Lord, for the blessings I receive
from my brothers and sisters in Christ.
Amen.

May 21

Praise

And Hezekiah appointed . . . the Levites . . .
to minister in the gates of the camp of the
Lord and to give thanks and praise.

2 Chron. 31:2, RSV

Proposal

Whenever you stand praying, forgive, if you
have anything against anyone; so that your
Father in heaven may also forgive you your
trespasses.

Mark 11:25, NRSV

Practice

Instead of nursing and rehearsing resentments, today I'll release them to the Lord
and forgive the perpetrators.

Promise

[Jesus said,] "The Counselor, the Holy Spirit,
. . . will teach you all things and will remind
you of everything I have said to you."

John 14:26, NIV

Prayer

Thank you, Lord, for revealing new insights
each day. Amen.

Praise

Seven times a day I praise thee
for thy righteous ordinances.

Ps. 119:164, RSV

Proposal

[Jesus said,] "Those who love me will keep
my word, and my Father will love them, and
we will . . . make our home with them."

John 14:23, NRSV

Practice

By attempting to view life from the other
person's perspective today, I'll obey the
Lord's commandment to love my neighbor.

Promise

God . . . bound himself with an oath, so that
those he promised to help would be perfectly sure and never need to wonder
whether he might change his plans. . . .
It is impossible for God to tell a lie.

Heb. 6:17-18, TLB

Prayer

Thank you, Lord, for your unchangeable
character and the security this gives me.
Amen.

Praise

His name will be proclaimed in Zion,
    and he will be praised in Jerusalem.

Ps. 102:21, TEV

Proposal

"Love the Lord your God with all your heart
and with all your soul and with all your
mind." This is the first and greatest commandment. And the second is like it: "Love
your neighbor as yourself."

Matt. 22:37-38, NIV

Practice

Today I'll meditate on God's Word and
commit portions of it to memory for future
reference.

Promise

You are precious in my eyes,
    and honored, and I love you.

Isa. 43:4, RSV

Prayer

Thank you, Lord, for your love and com-
panionship. Amen.

Praise

I face your holy Temple,
    bow down, and praise your name
because of your constant love and
        faithfulness.

Ps. 138:2, TEV

Proposal

Let the giving of thanks be your sacrifice
        to God,
and give the Almighty all that you promised.

Ps. 50:14, TEV

Practice

Today I'll press on toward good health by
caring for my body, developing my mind,
and growing closer to the Lord.

Promise

"Where, O death is your victory?
    Where, O death is your sting?" . . .
Thanks be to God! He gives us the victory
through our Lord Jesus Christ.

1 Cor. 15:55, 57, NIV

Prayer

Thank you, Lord, for conquering death and
thus banishing my fear of death. Amen.

Praise

Sing praises to the Lord, enthroned in Zion;
>   proclaim among the nations what
>   he has done.

Ps. 9:11, NIV

Proposal

Don't pay back a bad turn by a bad turn, to
anyone. Don't say, "It doesn't matter what
people think," but see that your public
behavior is above criticism.

Rom. 12:17, Phillips

Practice

If my emotional network is overloaded with
insensitive remarks or actions from others
today, I'll not retaliate in any fashion.

Promise

When we cry, "Abba, Father!" it is that very
Spirit bearing witness with our spirit that we
are children of God.

Rom. 8:15-16, NRSV

Prayer

Thank you, Lord, for the assurance that my
entrance into heaven is absolutely certain.
Amen.

May 26

Praise

With praise and thanksgiving they sang
   to the Lord: "He is good;
      his love to Israel endures forever."

Ezra 3:11, NIV

Proposal

If you forgive other people their failures,
your Heavenly Father will also forgive you.
But if you will not forgive other people,
neither will your Father forgive you your
failures.

Matt. 6:14-15, Phillips

Practice

I'll forgive those who have spoken unkindly
toward me by praying for their well-being
today.

Promise

I have loved you with an everlasting love;
   therefore I have continued my
      faithfulness to you.

Jer. 31:3, RSV

Prayer

Thank you, Lord, for promising to love me
forever. Amen.

Praise

From birth I have relied on you;
   you brought me forth from
     my mother's womb.
   I will ever praise you.

Ps. 71:6, NIV

Proposal

Give thanks to God, and so worship him as
he would be worshipped, with reverence
and awe.

Heb. 12:28-29, NEB

Practice

Today I'll mentally construct a list of blessings and joyfully praise the Lord for each
one.

Promise

The Spirit helps us in our weakness; for we
do not know how to pray as we ought, but
that very Spirit intercedes with sighs too
deep for words.

Rom. 8:26, NRSV

Prayer

Thank you, Lord, for your Spirit's wonderful
help when I pray. Amen.

Praise

I will praise thee, O Lord,
  with my whole heart;
I will show forth all thy marvelous works.

Ps. 9:1, KJV

Proposal

Listen, all of you. Love your *enemies.* Do *good* to those who *hate* you. . . . Implore God's blessing on those who *hurt* you.

Luke 6:27-28, TLB

Practice

Today I'll pray specifically for those who have ill feelings toward me or harm me in any way.

Promise

"I know the plans I have for you," declares the Lord, "plans to prosper you and not to harm you, plans to give you hope and a future."

Jer. 29:11, NIV

Prayer

Thank you, Lord, for enabling me to love my enemies and to hope in the future you are bringing. Amen.

Praise

King Hezekiah . . . ordered the Levites to praise the Lord. . . . So they sang praises with gladness and bowed their heads and worshiped.

2 Chron. 29:30, NIV

Proposal

Our Father in heaven . . .
> Forgive us the wrongs we have done,
> > as we forgive the wrongs
> > > that others have done to us.

Matt. 6:9, 12, TEV

Practice

Today I'll approach everyone with an attitude of forgiveness, understanding, and acceptance.

Promise

You too have been stamped with the seal of the Holy Spirit . . . which brings freedom for those whom God has taken for his own.

Eph. 1:13-14, JB

Prayer

Thank you, Lord, for the privilege of living a Spirit-filled life. Amen.

Praise

The six sons of Jeduthun . . . proclaimed
God's message, accompanied by the music
of harps, and sang praise and thanks to
the Lord.

1 Chron. 25:3, TEV

Proposal

Jesus said to [Peter], "Simon son of John,
do you love me more than these? . . .
Feed my lambs. . . .
Do you love me? . . . Tend my sheep. . . .
Do you love me? . . . Feed my sheep."

John 21:15-17, NRSV

Practice

Today I'll be sensitive to the needs of others
and willing to help at a moment's notice.

Promise

You will keep on guiding me all my life with
your wisdom and counsel; and afterwards
receive me into the glories of heaven!

Ps. 73:24, TLB

Prayer

Thank you, Lord, for never withholding
your Spirit from me. Amen.

May 31

Praise

One generation shall praise thy works
    to another,
   and shall declare thy mighty acts.

Ps. 145:4, KJV

Proposal

The sacrifice acceptable to God is
    a broken spirit;
   a broken and contrite heart, O God,
    thou wilt not despise.

Ps. 51:17, RSV

Practice

Today I'll place myself under control of the
Holy Spirit and praise the Lord in all things.

Promise

He will wipe away all tears from their eyes.
There will be no more death, no more grief
or crying or pain. The old things have dis-
appeared.

Rev. 21:4, TEV

Prayer

Thank you, Lord, for being the way to
heaven and providing the means for
abundant living. Amen.

June 1

Praise

The poor shall eat and be satisfied;
    all who seek the Lord shall find him
      and shall praise his name.
Their hearts shall rejoice with
    everlasting joy.

Ps. 22:26, TLB

Proposal

You get no credit for being patient if you are beaten for doing wrong; but if you do right and suffer for it, and are patient beneath the blows, God is well pleased.

1 Pet. 2:20, TLB

Practice

Today I'll practice patience by seeing the hand of the Lord in all circumstances.

Promise

[The Lord] will love you and bless you. . . . You will be blessed more than any other people.

Deut. 7:13-14, NIV

Prayer

Thank you, Lord, for enabling me to fellowship with you. Amen.

June 2

Praise

In God we make our boast all day long,
   and we will praise your name forever.

Ps. 44:8, NIV

Proposal

If you keep my commandments, you will
abide in my love, just as I have kept my
Father's commandments.

John 15:10, NRSV

Practice

Today I'll love my enemies by forgiving
them unconditionally and praying for their
well-being.

Promise

Who dares accuse us whom God has
chosen for his own? Will God? No! . . . Will
Christ? *No!* For he is . . . sitting at the place
of highest honor next to God, pleading for
us there in heaven.

Rom. 8:33-34, TLB

Prayer

Thank you, Lord Jesus, for interceding on
my behalf and making me your heir. Amen.

June 3

Praise

O Lord, open thou my lips;
    and my mouth shall show forth thy praise.

Ps. 51:15, KJV

Proposal

All of you serve each other with humble
spirits, for God gives special blessings to
those who are humble, but sets himself
against those who are proud.

1 Pet. 5:5, TLB

Practice

Today I'll prevent pride from robbing me of
joy by practicing humility in every event
and relationship.

Promise

The blood of Jesus, his Son, purifies us from
all sin.

1 John 1:7, NIV

Prayer

Thank you, Lord, for the blood of Jesus,
which frees me from the penalty of sin and
assures me of victory over death. Amen.

Praise

It is the living who praise you,
    As I praise you now.
Fathers tell their children
    how faithful you are.

Isa. 38:19, TEV

Proposal

Love your enemies, do good to them, and
lend to them without expecting to get any
thing back.

Luke 6:35, NIV

Practice

Today I'll love my enemies by treating them
with compassion, remembering my own
temptations and shortcomings.

Promise

Because you are children, God has sent the
Spirit of his Son into our hearts, crying,
"Abba! Father!"

Gal. 4:6, NRSV

Prayer

Thank you, Lord, for the Holy Spirit, who
empowers us to do your will and claim you
as our dear Father. Amen.

Praise

I have set the Lord continually before me:
    with him at my right hand
        I cannot be shaken.
Therefore my heart exults
    and my spirit rejoices.

Ps. 16:8-9, NEB

Proposal

You shall not covet your neighbor's house;
you shall not covet your neighbor's wife,
or male or female slave, or ox, or donkey,
or anything that belongs to your neighbor.

Exod. 20:17, NRSV

Practice

Today I refuse to nurse desire for my
neighbor's possessions or spouse.

Promise

Fear not, little flock, for it is your Father's
good pleasure to give you the kingdom.

Luke 12:32, RSV

Prayer

Thank you, Lord, for revealing yourself and
permitting me to fellowship with you each
day. Amen.

Praise

The Lord is my strength and my shield;
my heart trusted in him, and I am helped:
therefore my heart greatly rejoiceth;
and with my song will I praise him.

Ps. 28:7, KJV

Proposal

Never envy the wicked! Soon they fade
away like grass and disappear. Trust in the
Lord instead.

Ps. 37:1-3, TLB

Practice

Should envious thoughts enter my mind
today, I'll quickly replace them with
promises from Scripture.

Promise

As you know [God] better, he will give you,
. . . everything you need for living a truly
good life.

2 Pet. 1:3, TLB

Prayer

Thank you, Lord, for the gift of your Spirit,
who fills my heart with joy. Amen.

Praise

Open to me the gates of righteousness:
I will go into them,
and I will praise the Lord.

Ps. 118:19, KJV

Proposal

As we have opportunity, let us do good to all
people, especially to those who belong to
the family of believers.

Gal. 6:10, NIV

Practice

If the temptation to withdraw within myself
entices me today, I'll resist it by willing
myself to be involved in the lives of others.

Promise

How great is the love the Father has
lavished on us, that we should be called
children of God!

1 John 3:1, NIV

Prayer

Thank you, Lord, for the privilege of being
grafted into your family. Amen.

Praise

My praise shall be of thee in the
  great congregation, [O Lord]:
I will pay my vows
  before them that fear him.

Ps. 22:25, KJV

Proposal

Since we live by the Spirit, let us keep in
step with the Spirit. Let us not become con-
ceited, provoking and envying each other.

Gal. 5:25 26, NIV

Practice

Today I simply refuse to entertain envious
or jealous thoughts.

Promise

There is now no condemnation for those
  who are in Christ Jesus,
because . . . the Spirit of life set me free
  from the law of sin and death.

Rom. 8:1-2, NIV

Prayer

Thank you, Lord, for providing the way to
victory over sin and death. Amen.

June 9

Praise

I call to the Lord, who is worthy of praise,
and I am saved from my enemies.

Ps. 18:3, NIV

Proposal

Do not take revenge
on someone who wrongs you.
If anyone slaps you on the right cheek,
let him slap your left cheek too.
And if someone takes you to court
to sue you for your shirt,
let him have your coat as well.

Matt. 5:39-40, TEV

Practice

Today I'll forgive those who wrong me, and
I'll pray for them.

Promise

You are my father and my God;
you are my protector and savior.

Ps. 89:26, TEV

Prayer

Thank you, Lord, for being whatever I need
when I open myself to you. Amen.

Praise

Then I will thank thee
> in the great congregation;
> in the mighty throng I will praise thee.

Ps. 35:18, RSV

Proposal

The point is this: the one who sows
sparingly will also reap sparingly, and the
one who sows bountifully will also reap
bountifully.

2 Cor. 9:6, NRSV

Practice

Today I'll be sensitive to the needs of others
and be willing to lend a helping hand.

Promise

Your Father already knows what you need
before you ask him.

Matt. 6:8, TEV

Prayer

Thank you, Lord, for fulfilling deep longings
that only you can satisfy. Amen.

June 11

Praise

Ye that fear the Lord, praise him;
    all ye the seed of Jacob, glorify him;
    and fear him, all ye the seed of Israel.

Ps. 22:23, KJV

Proposal

And the Lord's servant must not be quarrel-
some but kindly to everyone . . . patient,
correcting opponents with gentleness. God
may perhaps grant that they will repent and
come to know the truth.

2 Tim. 2:24-25, NRSV

Practice

Today I'll be kind to everyone I meet and
be careful to avoid squabbles.

Promise

Your sins have been forgiven in the name
of Jesus our Savior.

1 John 2:12, TLB

Prayer

Thank you, Lord, for providing a solution to
my bent to quarrel and to be impatient.
Amen.

June 12

Praise

And now shall mine head be lifted up
     above mine enemies round about me . . .
I will sing, yea, I will sing praises
     unto the Lord.

Ps. 27:6, KJV

Proposal

This is love for God: to obey his commands.
And his commands are not burdensome,
for everyone born of God overcomes the
world.

1 John 5:3-4, NIV

Practice

Today I'll obey the commands of God and
resist the temptations of Satan.

Promise

His anger lasts a moment;
     his favor lasts for life!
Weeping may go on all night,
     but in the morning there is joy.

Ps. 30:5, TLB

Prayer

Thank you, Lord, for your favor, which comforts me in the midst of sorrow. Amen.

June 13

Praise

I will tell of your name
>   to my brothers and sisters;
>   in the midst of the congregation
>   I will praise you.

Ps. 22:22, NRSV

Proposal

Stop doing wrong, learn to do right!
>   Seek justice, encourage the oppressed.
Defend the cause of the fatherless,
>   plead the case of the widow.

Isa. 1:16-17, NIV

Practice

Today I'll pray specifically for my
acquaintances who are widows and children without fathers.

Promise

"I will be a Father to you,
>   and you will be my sons and daughters,"
>   says the Lord Almighty.

2 Cor. 6:18, NIV

Prayer

Thank you, Lord, for adopting me into your
family and being our Father. Amen.

June 14

Praise

When I remember these things,
   I pour out my soul in me . . .
I went with them to the house of God,
   with the voice of joy and praise,
   with a multitude that kept holyday.

Ps. 42:4, KJV

Proposal

Don't quarrel with anyone. Be at peace with
everyone, just as much as possible.

Rom. 12:18, TLB

Practice

Today I'll place the needs of others ahead of
my own, and I'll remember joining with
others in joyful worship of God.

Promise

He is able to save completely those who
come to God through him, because he
always lives to intercede for them.

Heb. 7:25, NIV

Prayer

Thank you, Lord Jesus, for interceding for
me. Amen.

Praise

I sing a hymn of thanksgiving. . . .
   In the assembly of his people
      I praise the Lord.

Ps. 26:7, 12, TEV

Proposal

The godly man gives generously to the
poor. His good deeds will be an honor to
him forever.

2 Cor. 9:9, TLB

Practice

Today I'll give to the poor, pray for them,
and lend a hand as opportunities arise.

Promise

Your ears will hear a voice behind you,
saying, "This is the way; walk in it."

Isa. 30:21, NIV

Prayer

Lord, without your presence, life would be
unbearable and unmanageable. Thank you
for promising always to guide me. Amen.

June 16

Praise

Wilt thou show wonders to the dead?
  Shall the dead arise and praise thee?

Ps. 88:10, KJV

Proposal

An offended [person] is more unyielding
    than a fortified city,
  and disputes are like the barred gates
    of a citadel.

Prov. 18:19, NIV

Practice

Today I'll be alert, in touch with everything
around me, and sensitive to my neighbor's
needs.

Promise

Jesus said, "Be sure of this—that I am with
you always, even to the end of the world."

Matt. 28:20, TLB

Prayer

Thank you, Lord Jesus, for the comfort of
knowing you are always with me, day and
night, anywhere. Amen.

Praise

I will not be silent:
    I will sing praise to you.
Lord, you are my God:
    I will give you thanks forever.

Ps. 30:12, TEV

Proposal

You shall rejoice in all the good things the
Lord your God has given to you and your
household.

Deut. 26:11, NIV

Practice

Today I'll make a conscious effort to praise
God in all things, even though I may not
feel like it.

Promise

[God's] eyes are upon the ways of mortals,
    and he sees all their steps.
There is no gloom of deep darkness
    where evildoers may hide themselves.

Job 34:21-22, NRSV

Prayer

Thank you, Lord, for protecting me from
evil schemes of wicked people. Amen.

June 18

Praise

In God will I praise his word:
   in the Lord will I praise his word. . . .
Thy vows are upon me O God:
   I will render praises unto thee.

Ps. 56:10, 12, KJV

Proposal

I give you a new commandment, that you
love one another. Just as I have loved you,
you also should love one another. By this
everyone will know that you are my disciples, if you have love for one another.

John 13:34-35, NRSV

Practice

Today I'll kneel to pray lovingly for those
who cause me heartache.

Promise

By day the Lord commands
      his steadfast love,
   and at night his song is with me.

Ps. 42:8, NRSV

Prayer

Thank you, Lord Jesus, for loving me so that
I can love others. Amen.

June 19

Praise

I will praise thee, O Lord my God,
   with all my heart:
and I will glorify thy name for evermore.

Ps. 86:12, KJV

Proposal

Pursue peace with everyone, and the holiness without which no one will see the Lord.

Heb. 12:14, NRSV

Practice

Today my first goal is to live in harmony with others. To make peace, I'm willing to do anything within God's purposes.

Promise

If you then . . . know how to give good gifts to your children, how much more will your Father in heaven give the Holy Spirit to those who ask him!

Luke 11:13, NIV

Prayer

Thank you, Lord, for filling me with your Spirit and thereby producing fruit in my life. Amen.

June 20

Praise

Sing unto God, sing praises to his name:
    extol him that rideth upon the heavens
        by his name JAH,
    and rejoice before him.

Ps. 68:4, KJV

Proposal

Love one another with mutual affection;
    outdo one another in showing honor.

Rom. 12:10, NRSV

Practice

Today I'll show respect and enthusiasm for
people, regardless of how they act.

Promise

If we love one another, God lives in union
with us, and his love is made perfect in us.

1 John 4:12, TEV

Prayer

Thank you, Lord, for your Spirit, who
enables me to overcome any obstacle.
Amen.

Praise

But I will rejoice for ever,
  I will sing praises to the God of Jacob.

Ps. 75:9, RSV

Proposal

Those who say, "I love God," and hate their brothers or sisters, are liars; for those who do not love [one] . . . whom they have seen, cannot love God whom they have not seen.

1 John 4:20, NRSV

Practice

I believe that in Christ I can choose and follow God's way—and today I choose to love people, regardless of their color, creed, or national origin.

Promise

I will deliver you out of the hand
      of the wicked,
  and redeem you from the grasp
      of the ruthless.

Jer. 15:21, NRSV

Prayer

Thank you, Lord, for delivering me and helping me love everyone I see. Amen.

Praise

They are the people I made for myself,
and they will sing my praises!

Isa. 43:21, TEV

Proposal

Be full of love for others, following the
example of Christ who loved you and gave
himself to God as a sacrifice to take away
your sins.

Eph. 5:2, TLB

Practice

Today I'll see people through the healthy
light of the Holy Spirit and treat them
accordingly.

Promise

I have told you this so that my joy may be in
you and that your joy may be complete.

John 15:11, NIV

Prayer

Thank you, Lord, for your joy, which
enriches my life beyond measure. Amen.

June 23

Praise

Let them praise the name of the Lord!
  For he commanded and they were created.

Ps. 148:5, RSV

Proposal

O Most High, when I am afraid,
  I put my trust in you.
In God, whose word I praise,
    in God I trust; I am not afraid;
    what can flesh do to me?

Ps. 56:2-4, NRSV

Practice

With the Lord by my side today, I refuse to
be intimidated.

Promise

Let us know, let us press on to know
      the Lord;
    his going forth is sure as the dawn;
he will come to us as the showers,
    as the spring rains that water the earth.

Hos. 6:3, RSV

Prayer

Thank you, Lord, for enabling me to go
beyond my usual limitations. Amen.

June 24

Praise

O God, it is right for us to praise you
    in Zion . . .

    because you answer prayers.
You show your care . . . by sending rain;
    you make [the land] rich and fertile.
Everything shouts and sings for joy.

Ps. 65:1, 9, 13, TEV

Proposal

Don't just pretend that you love others:
really love them. I hate what is wrong. Stand
on the side of the good.

Rom. 12:9, TLB

Practice

Today I'll display love for others by being
kind, considerate, and courteous in every
situation.

Promise

[God] will always make you rich enough to
be generous at all times.

2 Cor. 9:11, TEV

Prayer

Thank you, Lord, for spiritual blessings that
come from giving to others. Amen.

June 25

Praise

Do not let the oppressed retreat in disgrace;
  may the poor and needy praise your name.

Ps. 74:21, NIV

Proposal

Above all, clothe yourselves with love,
which binds everything together in perfect
harmony.

Col. 3:14, NRSV

Practice

Today I'll be friendly, open, warm, and
interested in others. I'll be a good listener.

Promise

He will cover you with his feathers,
    and under his wings you will find
        refuge. . . .
You will not fear the terror of night . . .
    nor the plague that destroys at midday.

Ps. 91:4-6, NIV

Prayer

Thank you, Lord, for being my refuge in
times of terror. Amen.

June 26

Praise

We will not hide them from their children,
  showing to the generation to come the
    praises of the Lord, and his strength,
and his wonderful works that he hath done.

Ps. 78:4, KJV

Proposal

No one should be looking to his own interests, but for the interests of others.

1 Cor. 10:24, TEV

Practice

Today I'll find joy and fulfillment in praising God and helping others.

Promise

No other nation, no matter how great, has a god who is so near when they need him as the Lord our God is to us.

Deut. 4:7, TEV

Prayer

Thank you, Lord, for never refusing to answer my cries for help. Amen.

Praise

Blessed are they that dwell in thy house:
  they will be still praising thee. Selah.

Ps. 84:4, KJV

Proposal

Let every person be subject to the govern-
ing authorities; for there is no authority
except from God, and those . . . that exist
have been instituted by God.

Rom. 13:1, NRSV

Practice

Today I'll cheerfully submit to all civil and
spiritual authority to which I'm accountable.

Promise

Jesus . . . said, "I am the light of the world.
Whoever follows me will never walk in darkness, but will have the light of life."

John 8:12, NIV

Prayer

Thank you, Lord, for the Scriptures, which
illuminate the way to abundant living.
Amen.

June 28

Praise

Then I will go to the altar of God,
    to God my exceeding joy;
and I will praise thee with the lyre,
    O God, my God.

Ps. 43:4, RSV

Proposal

A relaxed attitude lengthens [one's] life;
    jealousy rots it away.

Prov. 14:30, TLB

Practice

If negative feelings arise today, I refuse to
let them lead to insecure thoughts.

Promise

I will restore to you the years
    which the swarming locust has eaten,
the hopper, the destroyer, and the cutter. . . .
You shall eat in plenty and be satisfied.

Joel 2:25-26, RSV

Prayer

Thank you, Lord, for the power to choose
thoughts and control impulses. Amen.

June 29

Praise

I will hope continually,
    and will praise thee yet more and more.

Ps. 71:14, RSV

Proposal

Whoever says, "I am in the light,"
    while hating a brother or sister,
        is still in the darkness.

1 John 2:9, NRSV

Practice

Today I'll practice the love of Christ by doing something beneficial for another human being.

Promise

[Jesus said,] "You will receive power when the Holy Spirit has come upon you; and you will be my witnesses . . . to the ends of the earth."

Acts 1:8, NRSV

Prayer

Thank you, Lord, for enabling me to share the good news of the gospel with others. Amen.

June 30

Praise

O God, my heart is quiet and confident.
  No wonder I can sing your praises!

Ps. 57:7, TLB

Proposal

Let your conversation be always full of
grace, seasoned with salt, so that you may
know how to answer everyone.

Col. 4:6, NIV

Practice

Today I refuse to lash out toward anyone in
anger or to pout or sulk in response to
irritations.

Promise

The joy of the Lord shall fill you full;
  you shall glory in the God of Israel.

Isa. 41:16, TLB

Prayer

Thank you, Lord, for the joy of devotions,
exercising, good food, friendships, and
family. Amen.

July 1

Praise

[May God] give you a spirit of unity among yourselves as you follow Christ Jesus, so that with one heart and mouth you may glorify the God and Father of our Lord Jesus Christ.

Rom. 15:5-6, NIV

Proposal

Make the most of your chances to tell others the good news. Be wise in all your contacts with them.

Col. 4:5, TLB

Practice

Today I'll make every effort to share my faith with another human being, with tact and respect.

Promise

So if the Son makes you free,
   you will be free indeed.

John 8:36, RSV

Prayer

Thank you, Lord, for your Spirit, who enables me to exchange disturbing thoughts for those of peace and contentment. Amen.

Praise

[The wise men said,] "Where is he who has been born king of the Jews? For we have seen his star in the East, and have come to worship him."
Matt. 2:2, RSV

Proposal

Do not show partiality to the poor or favoritism to the great, but judge your neighbor fairly.
Lev. 19:15, NIV

Practice

Today I'll make every effort to treat each person with respect and kindness.

Promise

[Jesus said,] "Everyone therefore who acknowledges me before others, I also will acknowledge before my Father in heaven."
Matt. 10:32, NRSV

Prayer

Thank you, Lord Jesus, for acknowledging me in heaven. Amen.

July 3

Praise
When they heard that the Lord was concerned about them and had seen their misery, they bowed down and worshiped.
Exod. 4:31, NIV

Proposal
Live as free people; do not, however, use your freedom to cover up any evil, but live as God's slaves.
1 Pet. 2:16, TEV

Practice
Today I'll examine my goals and discard those not motivated by love.

Promise
[The Lord] restores my soul.
He leads me in paths of righteousness
   for his name's sake.
Ps. 23:3, RSV

Prayer
Thank you, Lord, for enabling me to deal successfully with life one day at a time. Amen.

July 4

Praise

Praise the Lord, you heavenly beings:
    praise his glory and power. . . .
The voice of the Lord is heard
    in all its might and majesty.

Ps. 29:1, 4, TEV

Proposal

Do everything without complaining or
arguing.

Phil. 2:14, NIV

Practice

Today I'll fulfill my responsibilities with
humility, cheerfulness, and a hopeful
attitude.

Promise

It is from God alone that you have your life
through Christ Jesus. . . . He made us pure
and holy and gave himself to purchase our
salvation.

1 Cor. 1:30, TLB

Prayer

Thank you, Lord Jesus, for sacrificing yourself to make me acceptable to God the
Father. Amen.

July 5

Praise

And Ezra said: "Thou art the Lord, thou alone; thou hast made heaven, the heaven of heavens, with all their host . . . and the host of heaven worships thee.

Neh. 9:6, RSV

Proposal

Do not judge others,
    and God will not judge you.

Luke 6:37, TEV

Practice

Today I choose not to act legalistically, self-righteously, or judgmentally toward anyone.

Promise

I am the Alpha and the Omega, the Beginning and the End. I will give water from the well of life free to anybody who is thirsty.

Rev. 21:6, JB

Prayer

Thank you, Lord, for the faith to see your kingdom and to experience the benefits thereof. Amen.

July 6

Praise
Who could ever give [the Lord] anything or lend him anything? All that exists comes from him; all is by him and for him. To him be glory for ever! Amen.

Rom. 11:35-36, JB

Proposal
Whatever you do, in word or deed, do everything in the name of the Lord Jesus, giving thanks to God the Father through him.

Col. 3:17, NRSV

Practice
Today I'll examine my motives and strive to obey the Lord, with thanksgiving.

Promise
[Jesus said,] "I am the vine, you are the branches. Those who abide in me and I in them bear much fruit, because apart from me you can do nothing."

John 15:5, NRSV

Prayer
Thank you, Lord, for grafting me to yourself so that I can share your love. Amen.

July 7

Praise

The heavens declare the glory of God;
 and the firmament showeth his handiwork.

Ps. 19:1, KJV

Proposal

Pray much for others. . . . Pray . . . for kings
and all others who are in authority over us,
or are in places of high responsibility, so
that we can live in peace and quietness.

1 Tim. 2:1-2, TLB

Practice

Today I'll pray for the goal of peace to be a
high priority of every world leader—*now!*

Promise

If we know that [God] hears us in whatever
we ask, we know that we have obtained the
requests made of him.

1 John 5:15, RSV

Prayer

Thank you, Lord, for never forsaking or
disappointing me. Amen.

July 8

Praise

Then I shall rejoice in the Lord
  and delight in his salvation.
My very bones cry out,
  "Lord, who is like thee?"

Ps. 35:9-10, NEB

Proposal

Conduct yourselves honorably among
[unbelievers], so that . . . they may see your
honorable deeds and glorify God when he
comes to judge.

1 Pet. 2:12, NRSV

Practice

Today I'll be trustworthy in relating with my
neighbors, without exception.

Promise

If we are children we are heirs as well: heirs
of God and coheirs with Christ, sharing his
sufferings so as to share his glory.

Rom. 8:17, JB

Prayer

Thank you, Lord, for counting me worthy to
share your sufferings. Amen.

Praise

They shall speak of the glory of
     your kingdom,
  and tell of your power,
to make known to all people
     your mighty deeds,
  and the glorious splendor of your kingdom.

Ps. 145:11-12, NRSV

Proposal

Submit yourselves to one another,
  because of your reverence for Christ.

Eph. 5:21, TEV

Practice

Today I'll joyfully submit to others, as suitable in God's eyes, for the primary purpose of promoting peace and harmony.

Promise

Blessed are the pure in heart,
  for they will see God.

Matt. 5:8, NRSV

Prayer

Thank you, Lord, for the clean, wholesome feeling that follows from having my sins forgiven. Amen.

July 10

Praise

When the crowds saw it, they were filled with awe, and they glorified God, who had given such authority to human beings.

Matt. 9:8, NRSV

Proposal

Support your faith with goodness, and goodness with knowledge . . . self-control . . . endurance . . . godliness . . . mutual affection, and . . . love.

2 Pet. 1:5-7, NRSV

Practice

Because each relationship is rewarding and important, today I'll be sincere, warm, and open with everyone who crosses my path.

Promise

[Jesus said,] "For where two or three are gathered in my name, there am I in the midst of them."

Matt. 18:20, RSV

Prayer

Thank you, Lord, for the power that results from gathering with others in prayer. Amen.

July 11

Praise

Give unto the Lord the glory due unto
    his name;
  worship the Lord in the beauty of holiness.

Ps. 29:2, KJV

Proposal

Do not withhold good from those
    to whom it is due,
  when it is in your power to do it.

Prov. 3:27, NRSV

Practice

Today I refuse to allow negative thinking to
divert me from being a blessing to people
in need.

Promise

For he will keep me safe beneath his roof
    in the day of misfortune;
he will hide me under the cover of his tent;
  he will raise me beyond reach of distress.

Ps. 27:5, NEB

Prayer

Thank you, Lord, for the joy that results
from following you. Amen.

Praise

The man knelt down and worshiped the Lord. He said, "Praise the Lord, the God of my master Abraham, who has faithfully kept his promise to my master."

Gen. 24:26-27, TEV

Proposal

Do not be anxious how you are to speak or what you are to say; for what you are to say will be given to you in that hour.

Matt. 10:19, RSV

Practice

Today I'll be anxious about nothing. If circumstances begin to overwhelm me, I'll counter by counting my blessings.

Promise

Then my enemies will turn back
    when I call for help.
  By this I will know that God is for me.

Ps. 56:9, NIV

Prayer

Thank you, Lord, for being gracious to me during times of strife. Amen.

July 13

Praise

[Jesus prayed,] "I brought glory to you here on earth by doing everything you told me to. And now, Father, reveal my glory as I stand in your presence, the glory we shared before the world began."

John 17:4-5, TLB

Proposal

Like good stewards of the manifold grace of God, serve one another with whatever gift each of you has received.

1 Pet. 4:10, NRSV

Practice

Today I'll show concern for others by listening with my heart as well as my head.

Promise

Jesus said, "If you hold to my teaching . . . you will know the truth, and the truth will set you free."

John 8:31-32, NIV

Prayer

Thank you, Lord, for protecting me from my greatest enemy—myself! Amen.

July 14

Praise

He did this so that all the nations of the earth will realize that Jehovah is the mighty God, and so that all of you will worship him forever.

Josh. 4:24, TLB

Proposal

You are to live clean, innocent lives as children of God in a dark world full of people who are crooked and stubborn.

Phil. 2:15, TLB

Practice

Today I refuse to allow the failings of others to distract me from maintaining a positive attitude.

Promise

You are my defender and protector;
    I put my hope in your promise.

Ps. 119:114, TEV

Prayer

Thank you, Lord, for the assurance that you will always fulfill your promise. Amen.

Praise

The voice of the Lord spins and topples
    the mighty oaks. It strips the forests bare.
    They whirl and sway beneath the blast.
But in his temple all are praising,
    "Glory, glory to the Lord."

Ps. 29:9, TLB

Proposal

In everything, do to others what you would
have them do to you, for this sums up the
Law and the Prophets.

Matt. 7:12, NIV

Practice

Today I'll find something good in everyone
I meet and have genuine interest in people.

Promise

There is in store for me the crown of
righteousness, which the Lord . . . will
award to me on that day.

2 Tim. 4:8, NIV

Prayer

Thank you, Lord, for the assurance that my
labor will always be fruitful. Amen.

July 16

Praise

All the nations—and you made each one—
    will come and bow before you, Lord,
        and praise your great and holy name.
For you are great, and do great miracles.
    You alone are God.

Ps. 86:9-10, TLB

Proposal

Self-control means controlling the tongue! A quick retort can ruin everything.

Prov 13:3, TLB

Practice

Today I'll curb my tongue by referring to this book and looking for humor in every situation.

Promise

I sought the Lord, and he answered me;
    he delivered me from all my fears.

Ps. 34:4, NIV

Prayer

Thank you, Lord, for a clean conscience, a sound mind, and a strong faith. Amen.

July 17

Praise

They sing a new song [to the Lamb]:
"You are worthy to take the scroll
and to open its seals,
for you were slaughtered
and by your blood you ransomed for God
saints from every tribe and language
and people and nation."

Rev. 5:9, NRSV

Proposal

Whatever happens, dear friends, be glad in the Lord.

Phil. 3:1, TLB

Practice

If negative thoughts enter my mind today, I'll replace them with promises from the Word of God.

Promise

I will heal my people and will let them enjoy abundant peace and security.

Jer. 33:6, NIV

Prayer

Thank you, Lord, for peace and joy coming from your Spirit dwelling within me. Amen.

July 18

Praise

All nations will remember the Lord.
> From every part of the world
> > they will turn to him;
> all races will worship him.

Ps. 22:27, TEV

Proposal

Whoever does not take up the cross and follow me is not worthy of me.

Matt. 10:38, NRSV

Practice

Today I'll deny selfish impulses and do that which is pleasing to the Lord.

Promise

The Lord is our protector and glorious king,
> blessing us with kindness and honor.
He does not refuse any good thing
> to those who do what is right.

Ps. 84:11, TEV

Prayer

Thank you, Lord, for loving me and granting the desires of my heart. Amen.

July 19

Praise

They will see the Son of man coming in clouds with great power and glory.

Mark 13:26, RSV

Proposal

For God has bought you with a great price. So use every part of your body to give glory back to God, because he owns it.

1 Cor. 6:20, TLB

Practice

Today I'll exercise, consume nutritious foods, and get plenty of rest.

Promise

He was pierced through for our faults,
    crushed for our sins.
On him lies a punishment
    that brings us peace,
and through his wounds we are healed.

Isa. 53:5, JB

Prayer

Thank you, Lord Jesus, for paying the penalty for my sin. Amen.

July 20

Praise

Then in my vision I heard the singing of
millions of angels surrounding the throne
and the Living Beings and the Elders:
"The Lamb is worthy."

Rev. 5:11, TLB

Proposal

With [the tongue] we bless the Lord and
Father. . . . From the same mouth [ought
not] come blessing and cursing.

Jas. 3:9-10, NRSV

Practice

Today I'll utter no remarks condemning
others and I won't encourage anyone who
says such things.

Promise

For the Lord is always good.
He is always loving and kind,
and his faithfulness goes on and on
to each succeeding generation.

Ps. 100:5, TLB

Prayer

Thank you, Lord, for your patience when I
deliberately disobey you. Amen.

Praise

Worship the Lord in the splendor
of his holiness;
tremble before him, all the earth.
Say among the nations, "The Lord reigns."

Ps. 96:9-10, NIV

Proposal

Strive to be found by [Christ] at peace,
without spot or blemish; and . . . grow in
the grace and knowledge of our Lord and
Savior Jesus Christ.

2 Pet. 3:14, 18, NRSV

Practice

Today I'll focus on obeying the Lord and
standing on his promises.

Promise

Thou preparest a table before me
in the presence of my enemies;
thou anointest my head with oil,
my cup overflows.

Ps. 23:5, RSV

Prayer

Thank you, Lord, for the tranquillity that
permeates my soul. Amen.

Praise

When the Son of Man comes in his glory,
and all the angels with him, then he will sit
on the throne of his glory.

Matt. 25:31, NRSV

Proposal

You shall not misuse the name of the Lord
your God, for the Lord will not hold anyone
guiltless who misuses his name.

Exod. 20:7, NIV

Practice

Today I'll do nothing to defame the name of
the Lord in any manner.

Promise

"For I am the Lord—I do not change. . . ,"
    says the Lord of Hosts.
"Come and I will forgive you."

Mal. 3:6-7, TLB

Prayer

Thank you, Lord, for being an unalterable
foundation for my life. Amen.

Praise

The Lord reigns, let the earth be glad;
   let the distant shores rejoice....
The heavens proclaim his righteousness,
   and all the peoples see his glory.

Ps. 97:1, 6, NIV

Proposal

"There is a saying, 'Love your *friends* and
hate your enemies.' But I say: Love your
enemies! Pray for those who *persecute* you!"

Matt. 5:43-44, TLB

Practice

Today I'll pray for anyone who might
persecute me, take me for granted,
or disappoint me.

Promise

This God . . . is the shield of all who take
refuge in him.

2 Sam. 22:31, JB

Prayer

Thank you, Lord, for your patience, faithfulness, and willingness to satisfy my needs.
Amen.

July 24

Praise

Be thou exalted, O God,
> above the heavens:
> and thy glory above all the earth.

Ps. 108:5, KJV

Proposal

No one can serve two masters; for a slave
will either hate the one and love the other,
or be devoted to the one and despise the
other. You cannot serve God and wealth.

Matt. 6:24, NRSV

Practice

Today I'll be neither a miser nor a spend-
thrift, but rather a prudent steward with
what the Lord has provided to me.

Promise

The Lord is merciful and loving,
> slow to become angry
> and full of constant love.

Ps. 103:8, TEV

Prayer

Thank you, Lord, for the joy and contentment that glows in the innermost recesses
of my soul. Amen.

Praise

Immediately he received his sight and followed Jesus, praising God. When all the people saw it, they also praised God.

Luke 18:43, NIV

Proposal

Without faith it is impossible to please God, for whoever would approach him must believe that he exists and that he rewards those who seek him.

Heb. 11:6, NRSV

Practice

Today I'll spend time seeking the Spirit's guidance and reaching out to others.

Promise

The Lord is a refuge for the oppressed, a place of safety in times of trouble.

Ps. 9:9, TEV

Prayer

Thank you, Lord, for the inner strength that results from me opening myself to you. Amen.

July 26

Praise

Moses made haste, and bowed his head
toward the earth, and worshiped.

Exod. 34:8, KJV

Proposal

Take your part in suffering, as a loyal soldier
of Christ Jesus.

2 Tim. 2:3, TEV

Practice

Regardless of the hand life deals me today,
I'll place the Lord Jesus on the throne of my
heart and life, and I'll receive the infilling of
the Holy Spirit.

Promise

Yes, grass withers and flowers fade,
    but the word of our God endures forever.

Isa. 40:8, TEV

Prayer

Thank you, Lord, for the Scriptures, whose
teachings and counsel are relevant to my
life and never out-of-date. Amen.

Praise

When Abraham's servant heard their words,
   he worshipped the Lord,
      bowing himself to the earth.

Gen. 24:52, KJV

Proposal

Everyone who looks at a woman with lust
has already committed adultery with her in
his heart.

Matt. 5:28, NRSV

Practice

Today I'll make every effort to focus
exclusively on positive, productive, and
secure thoughts.

Promise

Wisdom will enter your heart, and
knowledge will be pleasant to your soul.

Prov. 2:10, NIV

Prayer

Thank you, Lord, for the wisdom to
understand spiritual truths that would
otherwise be too deep for me. Amen.

Praise

Job got up and tore his robe and shaved his head. Then he fell to the ground to worship:
. . . "Naked I came from my mother's womb, and naked I will depart.
The Lord gave and the Lord has taken away; may the name of the Lord be praised."

Job 1:20-21, NIV

Proposal

Remember the sabbath day, to keep it holy. Six days you shall labor, and do all your work.

Exod. 20:8-9, RSV

Practice

Except for an emergency, I'll rest one day out of every seven.

Promise

[The Lord said,]
    "I will be true and faithful; . . .
        and make you mine forever."

Hos. 2:19, TEV

Prayer

Thank you, Lord, for bonding me to yourself. Amen.

July 29

Praise

[Many angels said] with a loud voice,
"Worthy is the Lamb that was slain
to receive power, and riches,
and wisdom, and strength, and honor,
and glory, and blessing."

Rev. 5:12, KJV

Proposal

If you are angry with a brother or sister, you
will be liable to judgment; and if you insult
a brother or sister, you will be liable to the
council; and if you say, "You fool," you will
be liable to the hell of fire.

Matt. 5:22, NRSV

Practice

Today I'll treat others respectfully regardless
of circumstances or how they deal with me.

Promise

[The Lord] heals the brokenhearted
and binds up their wounds.

Ps. 147:3, NIV

Prayer

Thank you, Lord, for comforting me when
I hurt. Amen.

July 30

Praise

I will praise you, O Lord,
  among the nations;
  I will sing of you among the peoples. . . .
Be exalted, O God, above the heavens,
  and let your glory be over all the earth.

Ps. 108:3, 5, NIV

Proposal

You shall not bear false witness against your
neighbor.

Exod. 20:16, RSV

Practice

Today I'll say nothing untrue about others,
and I will not listen to any gossip, regardless
of how tempting it may be.

Promise

If anyone is in Christ, there is a new creation: everything old has passed away; see,
everything has become new!

2 Cor. 5:17, NRSV

Prayer

Thank you, Lord, for new direction, insight,
values, priorities, and possibilities. Amen.

Praise

And Jehoshaphat bowed his head with his face to the ground: and all Judah and the inhabitants of Jerusalem fell before the Lord, worshipping the Lord.

2 Chron. 20:18, KJV

Proposal

Forgive, and you will be forgiven.

Luke 6:37, RSV

Practice

Today I refuse to develop a resentment toward anyone. I'll go to any lengths and do whatever it takes to turn the other cheek.

Promise

For the Lord watches over
    the way of the righteous,
  but the way of the wicked will perish.

Ps. 1:6, NIV

Prayer

Thank you, Lord, for loving me in spite of my shortcomings and defects of character. Amen.

August 1

Praise

Everyone who was there joined in worship,
and the singing and the rest of the music
continued until all the sacrifices had been
burned. Then King Hezekiah and all the
people knelt down and worshiped God.

2 Chron. 29:28-29, TEV

Proposal

Be of good courage,
and he shall strengthen your heart,
all ye that hope in the Lord.

Ps. 31:24, KJV

Practice

Today I refuse to permit disturbing
thoughts to disrupt my fellowship with the
Lord.

Promise

The Lord redeems his servants;
no one who takes refuge in him
will be condemned.

Ps. 34:22, NIV

Prayer

Thank you, Lord, for being my refuge in
times of trouble. Amen.

Praise

O Lord our God,
    other lords besides thee
        have ruled over us,
    but thy name alone we acknowledge.

Isa. 26:13, RSV

Proposal

[Jesus said,] "Whoever does not carry the
cross and follow me cannot be my disciple.
For which of you, intending to build a
tower, does not first sit down and estimate
the cost?"

Luke 14:27-28, NRSV

Practice

Today I'll resist the temptation to place selfish desires ahead of the needs of others.

Promise

You who live in the shelter of
        the Most High . . .
    abide in the shadow of the Almighty.

Ps. 91:1-2, NRSV

Prayer

Thank you, Lord, for always lifting my spirits
when I worship and praise you. Amen.

August 3

Praise

Blessed be the Lord, the God of Israel,
from everlasting to everlasting.

Ps. 41:13, NEB

Proposal

Whoever says something against the Holy
Spirit will not be forgiven—now or ever.

Matt. 12:32, TEV

Practice

Today I refuse to grieve the Holy Spirit in
thought, word, or deed.

Promise

They cried to the Lord in their trouble,
and he saved them from their distress.
He sent forth his word and healed them;
he rescued them from the grave.

Ps. 107:19-20, NIV

Prayer

Thank you, Lord, for calming my racing
imagination during times of emotional
upheaval. Amen.

August 4

Praise

They raise their voices, they shout for joy;
    from the west they acclaim
        the Lord's majesty.
Therefore in the east give glory to the Lord;
    exalt the name of the Lord,
        the God of Israel,
    in the islands of the sea.

Isa. 24:14-15, NIV

Proposal

Sing psalms, hymns, and sacred songs; sing to God with thanksgiving in your hearts.

Col. 3:16, TEV

Practice

Today I'll be especially grateful for ordinary blessings I normally take for granted.

Promise

The Lord will keep you safe.
    He will not let you fall into a trap.

Prov. 3:26, TEV

Prayer

Thank you, Lord, for helping me keep a joyful attitude during times of testing. Amen.

Praise

At that time the sign of the Son of Man will appear in the sky, and all the nations of the earth will . . . see the Son of Man coming in the clouds of the sky, with power and great glory.

Matt. 24:30, NIV

Proposal

These people honor me with their lips,
    but their hearts are far from me.

Matt. 15:8, NIV

Practice

Today I'll take a moral inventory, confess my sins, and work on overcoming my shortcomings.

Promise

Many are the afflictions of the righteous;
    but the Lord rescues them from them all.

Ps. 34:19, NRSV

Prayer

Thank you, Lord, for insights you reveal during times of suffering. Amen.

Praise

Behold, Jesus met them and said, "Hail!"
And they came up and took hold of his feet
and worshiped him.

Matt. 28:9, RSV

Proposal

If love can persuade at all, . . . then be
united in your convictions and united in
your love, with a common purpose.

Phil. 2:1-2, JB

Practice

Today I'll be sensitive to the feelings and
needs of others and as helpful as possible.

Promise

If you make the Most High
        your dwelling—. . .
    then no harm will befall you. . . .
He will command his angels
        concerning you
    to guard you in all your ways.

Ps. 91:9-11, NIV

Prayer

Thank you, Lord, for angels who watch over
me. Amen.

Praise

Exalt the Lord our holy God!
 Bow low before his feet.

Ps. 99:5, TLB

Proposal

Putting away falsehood, let all of us speak
the truth to our neighbors, for we are mem-
bers of one another.

Eph. 4:25, NRSV

Practice

Today I'll tell the truth in every situation,
regardless of the consequences.

Promise

The God who made both earth and heaven,
 . . . who keeps every promise . . .
 gives justice to the poor and oppressed,
 and food to the hungry. . . .
He lifts the burdens from those
 bent down beneath their loads.

Ps. 146:6-8, TLB

Prayer

Thank you, Lord, for providing for me,
either directly or through others, when I'm
incapable of providing for myself. Amen.

Praise

One of them, when he saw he was healed, came back, praising God in a loud voice. He threw himself at Jesus' feet and thanked him—and he was a Samaritan.

Luke 17:15-16, NIV

Proposal

Give thanks in all circumstances; for this is the will of God in Christ Jesus for you.

1 Thess. 5:18, NRSV

Practice

Today I'll approach every situation with a grateful heart and a positive attitude.

Promise

Give your burdens to the Lord.
    He will carry them.
He will not permit the godly to slip or fall.

Ps. 55:22, TLB

Prayer

Thank you, Lord, for teaching me to be content in any situation. Amen.

August 9

Praise

His work is honorable and glorious:
    and his righteousness endureth for ever.

Ps. 111:3, KJV

Proposal

[Jesus said,] "Not every one who says to me,
'Lord, Lord,' shall enter the kingdom of
heaven, but only the one who does the will
of my Father in heaven."

Matt. 7:21, NRSV

Practice

Today I'll seek the Lord's will for my life and
pray for the resolve to carry it out.

Promise

Surely goodness and love will follow me
    all the days of my life,
and I will dwell in the house of the Lord
    forever.

Ps. 23:6, NIV

Prayer

Thank you, Lord, for giving me the absolute
assurance of spending eternity with you.
Amen.

Praise

Ezra blessed the Lord, the great God. And all the people answered, "Amen, Amen," with lifting up their hands: and they bowed their heads, and worshipped the Lord with their faces to the ground.

Neh. 8:6, KJV

Proposal

Blind Pharisees! First cleanse the inside of the cup, and then the whole cup will be clean.

Matt. 23:26, TLB

Practice

Today I'll focus on improving my conscious contact with God.

Promise

The power of the wicked will be broken,
    but the Lord upholds the righteous.

Ps. 37:17, NIV

Prayer

Thank you, Lord, for revealing your will one day at a time. Amen.

August 11

Praise

[Saul said,] "Return with me, that I may worship the Lord your God." So Samuel turned back after Saul; and Saul worshiped the Lord.

1 Sam. 15:30-31, RSV

Proposal

As God's chosen people, holy and dearly loved, clothe yourselves with compassion, kindness, humility, gentleness and patience.

Col. 3:12, NIV

Practice

Today I'll be kind to others, regardless of how they treat me.

Promise

The meek shall possess the land,
    and delight themselves in abundant
        prosperity.

Ps. 37:11, RSV

Prayer

Thank you, Lord, for enabling me to maintain a patient attitude regardless of circumstances. Amen.

August 12

Praise

At once the man got up in front of them all, took the bed he had been lying on and went home, praising God. They were all completely amazed! Full of fear, they praised God.

Luke 5:25-26, TEV

Proposal

Pray at all times in the Spirit, with all prayer and supplication.

Eph. 6:18, RSV

Practice

Today I'll make it my business to obey the Lord, depend on him, and thank him for my blessings.

Promise

For as high as the heavens are above
> the earth,
so great is his love for those who fear him.

Ps. 103:11, NIV

Prayer

Thank you, Lord, for your support that creates and bolsters my inner security. Amen.

August 13

Praise

[The multitude] shouted aloud, "Victory to
our God, who sits on the throne,
and to the Lamb!"

Rev. 7:10, JB

Proposal

Wait for the Lord;
be strong, and let your heart take courage;
wait for the Lord!

Ps. 27:14, NRSV

Practice

If my faith is tested today, I won't seek an
easier way. Instead, I'll be victorious by per-
severing and trusting the Lord.

Promise

You love righteousness and hate
wickedness;
therefore God, your God, has set you
above your companions
by anointing you with the oil of joy.

Ps. 45:7, NIV

Prayer

Thank you, Lord, for the peace and joy that
rule my life. Amen.

Praise

All righteous people will rejoice
    because of what the Lord has done.
They will find safety in him;
    all good people will praise him.

Ps. 64:10, TEV

Proposal

On the outside you appear to people as
righteous but on the inside you are full of
hypocrisy and wickedness.

Matt. 23:28, NIV

Practice

Today I refuse to allow the failings of others
to distract me from maintaining a basic
attitude of joy in the Lord.

Promise

Those who sow tears shall reap joy.

Ps. 126:5, TLB

Prayer

Thank you, Lord, for helping me through
those dark nights of the soul when I have
teetered on the brink of despair. Amen.

August 15

Praise
He brought me by the way of the north gate to the front of the temple; and I looked, and behold the glory of the Lord filled the temple of the Lord; and I fell upon my face.

Ezek. 44:4, RSV

Proposal
Do not desire what belongs to someone else.

Rom. 7:7, TEV

Practice
Instead of longing for things I don't have, today I'll reflect upon the things I do have and thank the Lord for them.

Promise
The righteous cry out, and the Lord
    hears them;
  he delivers them from all their troubles.

Ps. 34:17, NIV

Prayer
Thank you, Lord, for these meditations, which constantly remind me to depend on you for every need. Amen.

Praise

It is good to give thanks to the Lord,
　　to sing praises to thy name, O Most High.

Ps. 92:1, RSV

Proposal

The Holy Spirit, God's gift, does not want
you to be afraid . . . to tell others about
our Lord.

2 Tim. 1:7-8, TLB

Practice

I know what I want today, and through the
power of the Holy Spirit, determination,
and a hopeful attitude, I'll obtain it.

Promise

But from everlasting to everlasting
　　the Lord's love is with those
　　　　who fear him.

Ps. 103:17, NIV

Prayer

Thank you, Lord, for the successes I've
enjoyed and also for the lessons I've
learned from failure. Amen.

August 17

Praise

"Now I will arise," says the Lord,
"now I will lift myself up;
now I will be exalted."

Isa. 33:10, NRSV

Proposal

This is the commandment, as you have heard from the beginning, that you follow love.

2 John 6, RSV

Practice

Today I'll treat people with love, respect, and compassion.

Promise

Has not God chosen the poor in the world to be rich in faith and to be heirs of the kingdom that he has promised to those who love him?

Jas. 2:5, NRSV

Prayer

Thank you, Lord, for the blessings of abundant living and the joy of sharing gifts with others. Amen.

Praise

God came from Teman,
the Holy One from Mount Paran. Selah.
His glory covered the heavens
and his praise filled the earth.

Hab. 3:3, NIV

Proposal

Fear God and give him glory . . .
worship him who made heaven and earth,
the sea and the fountains of water.

Rev. 14:7, RSV

Practice

Today I'll avoid defeat by praising God and
refusing to allow negative, destructive
thoughts to poison my mind.

Promise

I love those who love me,
and those who seek me find me.

Prov. 8:17, NIV

Prayer

Thank you, Lord, for enabling me to turn
bad breaks into advantages by seeing good
in every situation. Amen.

Praise

When [God] brings his firstborn into the
world, he says,
   "Let all God's angels worship him. . . ."
Of the Son he says,
   "Thy throne, O God, is for ever and ever."

Heb. 1:6, 8, RSV

Proposal

My child, be strong in the grace that is in
Christ Jesus.

2 Tim. 2:1, NRSV

Practice

If adversities cross my path today, I'll face
them head-on and search for opportunities
to realize even greater benefits.

Promise

If they obey and serve [God],
   they shall spend their days in prosperity,
      and their years in pleasures.

Job 36:11, KJV

Prayer

Thank you, Lord, for the resource of prayer
and the blessings I receive from communion with you. Amen.

Praise

Sing for joy to the Lord, all the earth;
    praise him with songs and shouts of joy!
Sing praises to the Lord!
    Play music on the harps!

Ps. 98:4-5, TEV

Proposal

Remind them . . . to speak evil of no one, to
avoid quarreling, to be gentle, and to show
every courtesy to everyone.

Titus 3:1-2, NRSV

Practice

Today I'll fill my mind with gentle thoughts
and surrender my will to the Lord.

Promise

When the ways of people please the Lord,
    he causes even their enemies to be
        at peace with them.

Prov. 16:7, NRSV

Prayer

Thank you, Lord, for the freedom to choose
which thoughts to keep and which to discard. Amen.

August 21

Praise

Jesus said, "I thank you, Father, Lord of heaven and earth, because you have hidden these things from the wise and the intelligent and have revealed them to infants, . . . for such was your gracious will."

Matt. 11:25-26, NRSV

Proposal

Examine yourselves to see whether you are in the faith; test yourselves. Do you not realize that Christ Jesus is in you?

2 Cor. 13:5, NIV

Practice

Today I refuse to allow arrogant, selfish thoughts to take control of my mind.

Promise

Though your sins be as scarlet,
   they shall be as white as snow;
though they be red like crimson,
   they shall be as wool.

Isa. 1:18, KJV

Prayer

Thank you, Lord, for providing a solution to the problem of sin. Amen.

August 22

Praise

[The angels, elders, and four living creatures worshiped God:] "Amen! Blessing and
glory and wisdom and thanksgiving and
honor and power and might be to our God
for ever and ever! Amen."

Rev. 7:11-12, RSV

Proposal

For the righteous will never be moved;
    they will be remembered forever.
They are not afraid of evil tidings;
    their hearts are firm, secure in the Lord.

Ps. 112:6-7, NRSV

Practice

Today I'll focus on trusting the Lord in spite
of many distractions.

Promise

For everyone who asks receives,
    and everyone who searches finds.

Luke 11:10, NRSV

Prayer

Thank you, Lord, for always delivering what
you promise. Amen.

August 23

Praise

The Levites . . . said,

> "Stand up and bless the Lord your God
>> from everlasting to everlasting.
> Blessed be thy glorious name which is
>> exalted above all blessing and praise."

Neb. 9:5, RSV

Proposal

Trust in the Lord with all your heart
> and lean not on your own understanding;
in all your ways acknowledge him,
> and he will make your paths straight.

Prov. 3:5-6, NIV

Practice

Today I'll acknowledge my weaknesses and rely on the Holy Spirit for power.

Promise

When the tempest passes,
> the wicked are no more,
> but the righteous are established forever.

Prov. 10:25, NRSV

Prayer

Thank you, Lord, for the opportunity to fellowship with you. Amen.

Praise

Whoever serves must do so with the strength that God supplies, so that God may be glorified in all things through Jesus Christ. To him belong the glory and the power for ever and ever. Amen.

1 Pet. 4:11, NRSV

Proposal

Beware! Don't always be wishing for what you don't have. For real life and real living are not related to how rich we are.

Luke 12:15, TLB

Practice

Today I'll enjoy the power of a contented attitude by trusting the Lord.

Promise

Be generous, and you will be prosperous. Help others, and you will be helped.

Prov. 11:25, TEV

Prayer

Thank you, Lord, for enabling me to persevere in spite of big obstacles. Amen.

August 25

Praise

You will hear people sing as they bring
thank offerings to my Temple; they will say,
"Give thanks to the Lord Almighty,
because he is good
and his love is eternal."

Jer. 33:11, TEV

Proposal

Are any among you suffering? They should
pray. Are any cheerful? They should sing
songs of praise.

Jas. 5:13, NRSV

Practice

Today I'll attract success by praising God
and maintaining a cheerful, trusting
attitude.

Promise

For the Lord giveth wisdom:
out of his mouth cometh knowledge
and understanding.

Prov. 2:6, KJV

Prayer

Thank you, Lord, for sustaining me through
adverse situations. Amen.

Praise

Be still, and know that I am God;
  I will be exalted among the nations,
  I will be exalted in the earth.

Ps. 46:10, NIV

Proposal

Do not be children in understanding;
however, in malice be babes, but in
understanding be mature.

1 Cor. 14:20, NKJB

Practice

Today I'll attempt to practice active listening, to listen for understanding rather than merely to be polite.

Promise

The righteous is delivered from trouble,
  and the wicked gets into it instead.

Prov. 11:8, RSV

Prayer

Thank you, Lord, for helping me in any
trouble and any difficult relationship,
through Christ. Amen.

August 27

Praise

Now I, Nebuchadnezzar, praise and glorify and honor the King of Heaven, the Judge of all, whose every act is right and good.

Dan. 4:37, TLB

Proposal

Show respect for everyone. Love Christians everywhere. Fear God and honor the government.

1 Pet. 2:17, TLB

Practice

Today I'll approach my work with joy and enthusiasm and go the extra mile without fanfare.

Promise

The fear of the Lord is
    the beginning of wisdom,
  and knowledge of the Holy One is
    understanding.

Prov. 9:10, NIV

Prayer

Thank you, Lord, for the wisdom and understanding that come from trusting you through bad times as well as good. Amen.

Praise

And they worshipped him . . . and were
continually in the temple, praising and
blessing God. Amen.

Luke 24:52-53, KJV

Proposal

Remind them to be submissive to rulers
and authorities, to be obedient, to be ready
for any honest work.

Titus 3:1, RSV

Practice

Today I'll obey the Lord and achieve victory
by working with enthusiasm, determination, and an attitude of blessing God.

Promise

[Jesus said,] "Those who love me will be
loved by my Father, and I will love them and
reveal myself to them."

John 14:21, NRSV

Prayer

Thank you, Lord, for granting wisdom that
can be obtained in no other way. Amen.

August 29

Praise

I will exalt you, O Lord,
for you lifted me out of the depths.

Ps. 30:1, NIV

Proposal

My righteous people, however,
will believe and live.

Heb. 10:38, TEV

Practice

Today I'll live a happy, love-filled life with a
positive attitude, attracting the good and
desirable and discarding the negative.

Promise

Your word is a lamp to my feet
and a light for my path.

Ps. 119:105, NIV

Prayer

Thank you, Lord, for the desire to achieve
Christ-centered goals and the tenacity to
keep trying in the midst of frustrating
circumstances. Amen.

August 30

Praise

Hallelujah!
   For our Lord God Almighty reigns.
Let us rejoice and be glad
   and give him glory!

Rev. 19:6-7, NIV

Proposal

The love of money is the first step toward all kinds of sin. Some people have even turned away from God because of their love of it.

1 Tim. 6:20, TLB

Practice

Today I'll conquer weakness by denying self, surrendering to God, and banishing selfish thoughts.

Promise

[The Lord says,] "Call to me and I will answer you and tell you great and unsearchable things you do not know."

Jer. 33:3, NIV

Prayer

Thank you, Lord, for enabling me to enjoy a thankful mental attitude, fixed on what is of eternal value. Amen.

Praise

[I saw those] victorious over the beast and his image. . . . They held harps given them by God and sang the song of Moses the servant of God and the song of the Lamb.

Rev. 15:2-3, NIV

Proposal

Through [Jesus Christ] then let us continually offer up a sacrifice of praise to God.

Heb. 13:15, RSV

Practice

Today I'll be generous and merciful in all my interactions with others and thus praise God with my life *and* my lips.

Promise

[God] does not take his eyes off the
      righteous;
   he enthrones them with kings
      and exalts them forever.

Job 36:7, NIV

Prayer

Thank you, Lord, for enabling me to accept things I cannot change. Amen.

September 1

Praise

Let the people of Sela sing for joy;
    let them shout from the mountaintops.
Let them give glory to the Lord
    and proclaim his praise in the islands.

Isa. 42:11-12, NIV

Proposal

Devote yourselves to prayer, being watchful and thankful.

Col. 4:2, NIV

Practice

Today I refuse to waste time yearning for a better future or reliving a glorious past. Instead, I'll make the most of the present by enjoying what I have.

Promise

If the Son therefore shall make you free,
    ye shall be free indeed.

John 8:36, KJV

Prayer

Thank you, Lord, for liberating me from the penalty and bondage of sin. Amen.

September 2

Praise

The four living creatures . . .
    never cease to sing,
 "Holy, holy, holy, is the Lord God Almighty,
    who was and is and is to come!"

Rev. 4:8, RSV

Proposal

Even if you are angry, you must not sin:
    never let the sun set on your anger.

Eph. 4:26, JB

Practice

Today I'll express my feelings without being
judgmental or displaying uncontrolled rage.

Promise

Whoever pursues righteousness and
        kindness
    will find life and honor.

Prov. 21:21, NRSV

Prayer

Thank you, Lord, for the power to replace
destructive thought patterns with holy ones
before the bad thoughts have a chance to
take root. Amen.

September 3

Praise

I knelt down and worshiped the Lord.
I praised the Lord, the God of my master
Abraham, who had led me.

Gen. 24:48, TEV

Proposal

You shall love your neighbor as yourself.

Matt. 22:39, RSV

Practice

Today I'll treat my neighbors with kindness
and respect, regardless of circumstances or
how they feel toward me.

Promise

Since by his blood he did all this for us as
sinners, how much more will he do for us
now that he has declared us not guilty? Now
he will save us from all of God's wrath to
come.

Rom. 5:9, TLB

Prayer

Thank you, Lord, for loving, accepting, and
forgiving me in spite of the mess I some-
times make of things. Amen.

September 4

Praise
Magi from the east came to Jerusalem and asked, "Where is the one who has been born king of the Jews? We saw his star in the east and have come to worship him."
Matt. 2:1-2, NIV

Proposal
First take the log out of your own eye, and then you will see clearly to take the speck out of your neighbor's eye.
Matt. 7:5, NRSV

Practice
If I am tempted to criticize or find fault with someone today, I'll look inward and make adjustments instead.

Promise
The fear of others lays a snare,
> but one who trusts in the Lord is secure.
Prov. 29:25, NRSV

Prayer
Thank you, Lord, for never betraying my trust in you. Amen.

Praise

The eleven disciples went away into
Galilee, into a mountain. . . . And when
they saw [Jesus], they worshipped him.
Matt. 28:16-17, KJV

Proposal

Clothe yourselves with humility toward one
another, because,
"God opposes the proud
but gives grace to the humble."
1 Pet. 5:5, NIV

Practice

Today I'll be sensitive to the feelings of
others rather than attempting to adjust
everything to suit my own desires.

Promise

Ask and it will be given to you;
seek and you will find;
knock and the door will be opened to you.
Luke 11:9, NIV

Prayer

Thank you, Lord, for increasing my capacity
to seek and find, and for decreasing my
limitations. Amen.

September 6

Praise

I will praise your power, Lord God;
　　I will proclaim your goodness, yours
　　　　alone. . . .
You have done great things;
　　there is no one like you.

Ps. 71:16, 19, TEV

Proposal

[Let] no one wrong or exploit a brother or
sister in this matter, because the Lord is an
avenger in all these things. . . . For God did
not call us to impurity but in holiness.

1 Thess. 4:6-7, NRSV

Practice

Today I'll attempt to view things from the
other person's perspective and treat others
as I'd like to be treated.

Promise

Those who trust in the Lord for help
　　will find their strength renewed.

Isa. 40:31, TEV

Prayer

Thank you, Lord, for rescuing me when
people or things disappoint me. Amen.

September 7

Praise

Sing for joy, O heavens . . .
   shout aloud, O earth beneath.
Burst into song, you mountains,
   you forests and all your trees,
for the Lord has redeemed Jacob,
   he displays his glory in Israel.

Isa. 44:23, NIV

Proposal

Let your manner of life be worthy of the
gospel of Christ.

Phil. 1:27, RSV

Practice

Today I'll spread cheer and goodwill to
everyone I meet.

Promise

If the Spirit of him who raised Jesus from
the dead dwells in you, he . . . will give life to
your mortal bodies also through his Spirit
that dwells in you.

Rom. 8:11, NRSV

Prayer

Thank you, Lord, for the glorious sense of
purpose in living for you. Amen.

Praise

I will shout for joy as I play for you;
  with my whole being I will sing
    because you have saved me.
I will speak of your righteousness
    all day long.

Ps. 71:23-24, TEV

Proposal

Come to terms quickly with your enemy
before it is too late.

Matt. 5:25, TLB

Practice

Today I'll face mistakes squarely, accept
responsibility for my actions, and seek
forgiveness from others when necessary.

Promise

No one who conceals transgressions
    will prosper,
  but one who confesses and
    forsakes them will obtain mercy.

Prov. 28:13, NRSV

Prayer

Thank you, Lord, for the wholeness I feel
after I confess my sins. Amen.

September 9

Praise

For you, O Lord, are good and forgiving,
abounding in steadfast love
to all who call on you.

Ps. 86:5, NRSV

Proposal

Peter . . . asked, "Lord, if [someone] keeps
on sinning against me, how many times do
I have to forgive?" . . . "Not seven times,"
answered Jesus, "but seventy times seven."

Matt. 18:21-22, TEV

Practice

Today I'll experience harmony and well-
being by forgiving those who have harmed
me.

Promise

We also rejoice in God through our Lord
Jesus Christ, through whom we have now
received reconciliation.

Rom. 5:11, NIV

Prayer

Thank you, Lord God, for developing the
forgiving heart of Jesus within me. Amen.

Praise

Let them thank the Lord . . .
    for his wonderful works to humankind.
Let them extol him in the congregation
    of the people, and
    praise him in the assembly of the elders.

Ps. 107:31-32, NRSV

Proposal

Strive for perfection; listen to my appeals;
agree with one another; live in peace.

2 Cor. 13:11, TEV

Practice

To everyone I meet today, I'll give a smile,
a word of encouragement, and a measure
of hope.

Promise

The kingdom of God is not a matter of
eating and drinking, but of righteousness,
peace and joy in the Holy Spirit.

Rom. 14:17, NIV

Prayer

Thank you, Lord, for the success that results
from trusting in you. Amen.

Praise

Be thou exalted, O God,
    above the heavens;
    let thy glory be above all the earth.

Ps. 57:5, KJV

Proposal

Be careful how you act; these are difficult
days. Don't be fools; be wise: make the
most of every opportunity you have for
doing good.

Eph. 5:15-16, TLB

Practice

If an opportunity to help someone presents
itself today, I'll follow through with action.

Promise

When you pass through the waters,
    I will be with you . . .
When you walk through the fire,
    you will not be burned.

Isa. 43:2, NIV

Prayer

Thank you, Lord, for enabling me to conquer fears and to seize opportunities for
doing good. Amen.

Praise

Those who were in the boat worshiped
[Jesus], saying, "Truly you are the Son
of God."

Matt. 14:33, NIV

Proposal

Be ye therefore merciful,
as your Father also is merciful.

Luke 6:36, KJV

Practice

Today I'll do something good for another
person with a cheerful, enthusiastic
attitude.

Promise

[Jesus said,] "I give [my sheep] eternal life,
and they shall never perish; no one can
snatch them out of my hand. My Father . . .
is greater than all; no one can snatch them
out of my Father's hand."

John 10:28-29, NIV

Prayer

Thank you, Lord, for keeping me in your
hand. Amen.

Praise

For you, O Lord, are the Most High
over all the earth;
you are exalted far above all gods.

Ps. 97:9, NIV

Proposal

Leave your gift there before the altar and
go; first be reconciled to your brother or
sister, and then come and offer your gift.

Matt. 5:24, NRSV

Practice

If I offend anyone today, I'll do everything
humanly possible to make amends before
the day is over.

Promise

Seek the Lord while he may be found;
call on him while he is near. . . .
You will go out in joy
and be led forth in peace.

Isa. 55:6, 12, NIV

Prayer

Thank you, Lord, for the rich, satisfying
relationship I enjoy with you every day.
Amen.

September 14

Praise

The kingdom of the world has become
the kingdom of our Lord
and of his Messiah,
and he will reign forever and ever.

Rev. 11:15, NRSV

Proposal

Don't cause the Holy Spirit sorrow by the
way you live.

Eph. 4:30, TLB

Practice

Today I'll walk in the power of the Holy
Spirit by facing reality boldly and looking
for good in every situation.

Promise

Jesus said to them, "I am the bread of life.
Whoever comes to me will never be hungry,
and whoever believes in me will never be
thirsty."

John 6:35, NRSV

Prayer

Thank you, Lord, for feeding me spiritually
even beyond my expectations. Amen.

Praise

My mouth will speak in praise of the Lord.
Let every creature praise his holy name
for ever and ever.

Ps. 145:21, NIV

Proposal

Stay away from the love of money;
be satisfied with what you have.

Heb. 13:5, TLB

Practice

If greedy thoughts enter my mind today, I'll
replace them by recalling at least five things
for which I'm grateful.

Promise

Since we have been justified through faith,
we have peace with God through our Lord
Jesus Christ.

Rom. 5:1, NIV

Prayer

Thank you, Lord, for the contentment that
results from surrendering my thoughts to
the control of the Holy Spirit. Amen.

September 16

Praise

Hallelujah! Yes, let his people praise him as they stand in his Temple courts.

Ps. 135:1-2, TLB

Proposal

The apostles gathered around Jesus, and . . . he said to them, "Come away to a deserted place all by yourselves and rest a while."

Mark 6:30-31, NRSV

Practice

If failure comes my way today, I refuse to wallow in regrets for past mistakes or lapse into discouragement and self-pity.

Promise

For in that He Himself, [God's Son,] has suffered, being tempted, He is able to aid those who are tempted.

Heb. 2:18, NKJB

Prayer

Thank you, Lord, for enabling me to overcome temptation. Amen.

September 17

Praise

Praise ye the Lord.
I will praise the Lord with my whole heart,
   in the assembly of the upright,
      and in the congregation.

Ps. 111:1, KJV

Proposal

Always give thanks for everything to our
God and Father in the name of our Lord
Jesus Christ.

Eph. 5:20, TLB

Practice

Today I'll replace disturbing thoughts with
secure ones that are hopeful and uplifting.

Promise

No eye has seen, nor ear has heard,
   no mind has conceived what God
      has prepared for those who love him.

1 Cor. 2:9, NIV

Prayer

Thank you, Lord, for the joy of knowing that
my place in eternity is absolutely secure.
Amen.

September 18

Praise

Shout with joy before the Lord, O earth!
Obey him gladly; come before him, singing
with joy.

Ps. 100:1-2, TLB

Proposal

Bless those who persecute you;
    bless and do not curse.

Rom. 12:14, NIV

Practice

If I am faced with differences of opinion or
misunderstandings today, I'll pray for the
other party and conduct a personal
inventory of myself.

Promise

We are ambassadors for Christ, since God is
making his appeal through us; we entreat
you on behalf of Christ, be reconciled
to God.

2 Cor. 5:20, NRSV

Prayer

Thank you, Lord, for making me your
ambassador and giving me a ministry of
reconciliation. Amen.

Praise

Praise the Lord with harp:
    sing unto him with the psaltery
        and an instrument of ten strings.
Sing unto him a new song.

Ps. 33:2-3, KJV

Proposal

My brothers and sisters, whenever you face trials of any kind, consider it nothing but joy.

Jas. 1:2, NRSV

Practice

If I experience failure today, I'll look for the cause within myself instead of blaming others.

Promise

[Jesus said,] "Where two or three come together in my name, there am I with them."

Matt. 18:20, NIV

Prayer

Thank you, Lord, for those who encourage me to develop character, exercise faith, and reach out to others in love. Amen.

September 20

Praise

I will sing of the mercies of the Lord
    for ever:
  with my mouth will I make known
    thy faithfulness to all generations.

Ps. 89:1, KJV

Proposal

Put to death . . . whatever belongs to your
earthly nature: sexual immorality, impurity,
lust, evil desires and greed, which is
idolatry.

Col. 3:5, NIV

Practice

Today I refuse to compromise my standards
through the self-justifying seduction of
rationalization.

Promise

The Lord will comfort his people.

Isa. 49:13, TEV

Prayer

Thank you, Lord, for enabling me to love
and respect myself in spite of many
shortcomings. Amen.

September 21

Praise

I will proclaim your name
>to my brothers and sisters,
in the midst of the congregation
>I will praise you.

Heb. 2:12, NRSV

Proposal

When others are happy, be happy with them. If they are sad, share their sorrow.

Rom. 12:15, TLB

Practice

Today I'll enhance my fellowship with the Lord by spending more energy on outside causes and less time on personal issues.

Promise

Anyone who believes and says that Jesus is the Son of God has God living in him, and he is living with God.

1 John 4:15, TLB

Prayer

Thank you, Lord, for the power to control my thoughts and make decisions. Amen.

September 22

Praise

I will sing to the Lord all my life;
   I will sing praise to my God
      as long as I live.

Ps. 104:33, NIV

Proposal

And do not get drunk with wine, for that is
debauchery; but be filled with the Spirit.

Eph. 5:18, RSV

Practice

Today I'll be able to handle whatever comes
along by relying on God's presence and a
thankful attitude.

Promise

The Spirit helps us in our weakness; for we
do not know how to pray as we ought, but
that very Spirit intercedes with sighs too
deep for words.

Rom. 8:26, NRSV

Prayer

Thank you, Lord, for enabling me to
develop the talent you gave me. Amen.

September 23

Praise

Praise ye the Lord.
> Praise, O ye servants of the Lord,
> praise the name of the Lord.

Ps. 113:1, KJV

Proposal

Thus says the Lord of hosts: Render true judgments, show kindness and mercy to one another.

Zech. 7:9, NRSV

Practice

Today I'll give a smile, kind word, sincere compliment, and encouragement to everyone with whom I come in contact.

Promise

To the one who pleases him
God gives wisdom and knowledge and joy.

Eccles. 2:26, NRSV

Prayer

Thank you, Lord, for helping me conserve valuable energy by not fretting over trivialities. Amen.

Praise

Make music to the Lord with the harp . . .
   with trumpets and the blast of the
     ram's horn—
   shout for joy before the Lord, the King.

Ps. 98:5-6, NIV

Proposal

My dear friend, do not imitate what is bad,
but imitate what is good.

3 John 11, TEV

Practice

Today I refuse to allow the memory of a
painful experience or failure to bind me in
a dark shroud of dejection and defeat.

Promise

Anyone united to the Lord becomes one
spirit with him.

1 Cor. 6:17, NRSV

Prayer

Thank you, Lord, for inner strength to pursue goals I establish through wise counsel
and prayer, rather than simply trying to
please others. Amen.

September 25

Praise

Be not silent, O God of my praise! . . .

> With my mouth I will give great thanks
> to the Lord;
> I will praise him in the midst of the throng.

Ps. 109:1, 30, RSV

Proposal

Don't be selfish; don't live to make a good impression on others. Be humble, thinking of others as better than yourself.

Phil. 2:3, TLB

Practice

Today I'll rely on renewed hope and determination to spark me to unselfish action.

Promise

Since he did not spare even his own Son for us but gave him up for us all, won't he also surely give us everything else?

Rom. 8:32, TLB

Prayer

Thank you, Lord, for helping me focus on blessings instead of troubles. Amen.

Praise

Let my mouth be filled with Your praise
    And with Your glory all the day.

Ps. 71:8, NKJB

Proposal

What good is it, my brothers and sisters, if
you say you have faith but do not have
works?

Jas. 2:14, NRSV

Practice

Today I'll make a list of possibilities that lie
before me, plan a course of action, and
begin with the most urgent.

Promise

God, who searches the heart, knows what is
the mind of the Spirit, because the Spirit
intercedes for the saints according to the
will of God.

Rom. 8:27, NRSV

Prayer

Thank you, Lord, for the visions I receive
and the guidance and inspiration to fulfill
them one day at a time. Amen.

Praise

I will sing of thy might;
  I will sing aloud of thy steadfast love
    in the morning. . . .
O my Strength, I will sing praises to thee.

Ps. 59:16-17, RSV

Proposal

Have the same concern for everyone. Do not be proud, but accept humble duties.

Rom. 12:16, TEV

Practice

If I receive criticism today, I'll separate honest concern from nit-picking and make adjustments.

Promise

The Lord will not forsake his people, . . . because it hath pleased the Lord to make you his people.

1 Sam. 12:22, KJV

Prayer

Thank you, Lord, for being my refuge in the midst of oppressive circumstances. Amen.

September 28

Praise
Praise the Lord,
    who carries our burdens day after day;
he is the God who saves us.
Ps. 68:19, TEV

Proposal
Live by the Spirit, and you will not gratify
the desires of the sinful nature.
Gal. 5:16, NIV

Practice
Today I'll experience victory over
temptation by relying on the Holy Spirit and
taking action when necessary.

Promise
Happy is the one
    who listens to me.
Prov. 8:34, NRSV

Prayer
Thank you, Lord, for the faith to see crises
as challenges to be conquered rather than
stumbling blocks to be feared. Amen.

September 29

Praise

Praise the Lord because he is so good;
   sing to his wonderful name.

Ps. 135:3, TLB

Proposal

Do not speak evil against one another,
brothers and sisters. Whoever speaks evil
against another or judges another, speaks
evil against the law; . . . if you judge the law,
you are not a doer of the law but a judge.

Jas. 4:11, NRSV

Practice

Today I'll search for any critical attitude
within me and neutralize it with prayer and
meditation.

Promise

Happy are those whose greatest desire
   is to do what God requires;
   God will satisfy them fully!

Matt. 5:6, TEV

Prayer

Thank you, Lord, for the satisfaction that
results from following you each day. Amen.

September 30

Praise

The Lord is great,
    and greatly to be praised. . . .
O worship the Lord
    in the beauty of holiness:
   fear before him, all the earth.

Ps. 96:4, 9, KJV

Proposal

Among you there must not be even a hint
of sexual immorality, or of any kind
of impurity, or of greed.

Eph. 5:3, NIV

Practice

If I feel some negative emotion creeping
over me today, I'll look within for the
problem and to the Lord for the solution.

Promise

Hope does not disappoint us, because God
has poured out his love into our hearts by
the Holy Spirit, whom he has given us.

Rom. 5:5, NIV

Prayer

Thank you, Lord, for your love that compels
me to love others. Amen.

October 1

Praise

All thy works shall praise thee, O Lord;
    and thy saints shall bless thee.

Ps. 145:10, KJV

Proposal

Who is wise and understanding among
you? Show by your good life that your works
are done with gentleness born of wisdom.

Jas. 3:13, NRSV

Practice

Today I'll put forth nothing less than maximum effort to reach my godly goals.

Promise

The Lord, your God, is in your midst . . .
    he will rejoice over you with gladness,
        he will renew you in his love.

Zeph. 3:17, RSV

Prayer

Thank you, Lord, for renewing my soul on
those occasions when I allow disturbing circumstances to drain me of joy and contentment. Amen.

October 2

Praise

As I learn your righteous judgments,
   I will praise you with a pure heart. . . .
I praise you, O Lord;
   teach me your ways.

Ps. 119:7, 12, TEV

Proposal

Obey God because you are his children;
don't slip back into your old ways—doing
evil because you knew no better.

1 Pet. 1:14, TLB

Practice

Today I will not let myself be enticed into
disobedience nor allow frustrating
experiences or negative people to rob me
of fellowship with God.

Promise

It is God himself who called you to share in
the life of his Son Jesus Christ our Lord; and
God keeps faith.

1 Cor. 1:9, NEB

Prayer

Thank you, Lord, for showing me your kingdom. Amen.

October 3

Praise

All the kings of the earth
        shall praise you, O Lord; . . .
They shall sing of the ways of the Lord,
    for great is the glory of the Lord.

Ps. 138:4-5, NRSV

Proposal

Beloved, do not grumble against one
another, so that you may not be judged.

Jas. 5:9, NRSV

Practice

If conflicts arise with others today, I'll look
for deficiencies within myself before doing
anything else.

Promise

The grass withereth, the flower fadeth:
    but the word of our God
        shall stand for ever.

Isa. 40:8, KJV

Prayer

Thank you, Lord, for the Scriptures, which
are relevant to life's problems in every age.
Amen.

Praise

Be exalted, O Lord, in your strength;
   we will sing and praise your might.

Ps. 21:13, NIV

Proposal

Love the Lord your God with all your heart,
with all your soul, with all your mind, and
with all your strength.

Mark 12:30, TEV

Practice

Today I'll express my love for the Lord by
spending time in prayer and lending an ear
to anyone who expresses a need.

Promise

The Lord is merciful and gracious,
   slow to anger
      and abounding in steadfast love.

Ps. 103:8, RSV

Prayer

Thank you, Lord, for the permanent and
unalterable things of life that bear witness
to your unchanging love. Amen.

October 5

Praise

It is not the dead who praise the Lord . . .
   It is we who extol the Lord,
      both now and forevermore.
Praise the Lord.

Ps. 115:17-18, NIV

Proposal

You must understand this, my beloved: let everyone be quick to listen, slow to speak, slow to anger; for your anger does not produce God's righteousness.

Jas. 1:19, NRSV

Practice

Today, regardless of my mood, I'll resist the temptation to speak spitefully.

Promise

We have not received the spirit of the world but the Spirit who is from God, that we may understand what God has freely given us.

1 Cor. 2:12, NIV

Prayer

Thank you, Lord, for the freedom to live as I choose—and I choose to live by your Spirit. Amen.

October 6

Praise

Great is the Lord,
> and greatly to be praised . . .
One generation shall praise thy works
> to another,
> and shall declare thy mighty acts.

Ps. 145:3-4, KJV

Proposal

Do not use your freedom as an opportunity
for self-indulgence, but through love
become slaves to one another.

Gal. 5:13, NRSV

Practice

Today I'll exercise a loving, respectful
attitude toward everyone who crosses my
path.

Promise

The Lord gives strength to his people;
> the Lord blesses his people with peace.

Ps. 29:11, NIV

Prayer

Thank you, Lord, for the spiritual truth and
intuition I receive each day. Amen.

Praise

Praise the Lord.
Praise the name of the Lord;
Praise him, you servants of the Lord.

Ps. 135:1, NIV

Proposal

Get rid of all that is wrong in your life, both inside and outside, and humbly be glad for the wonderful message we have received, for it is able to save.

Jas. 1:21, TLB

Practice

Today I'll banish disturbing thoughts by filling my mind with promises from the Word of God.

Promise

Turn to me and have mercy on me,
as you always do
to those who love your name.

Ps. 119:132, NIV

Prayer

Thank you, Lord, for flooding my soul with peace and teaching me to be content. Amen.

October 8

Praise

Praise ye the Lord.
Praise the Lord, O my soul.

Ps. 146:1, KJV

Proposal

Beloved, let us love one another; because
love is from God; everyone who loves is
born of God and knows God.

1 John 4:7, NRSV

Practice

Today I'll help people increase their self-
esteem by handing out sincere compli-
ments and recognizing positive aspects of
their lives.

Promise

I have revealed and saved and proclaimed.
. . . Yes, and from ancient days I am [God].
No one can deliver out of my hand.
When I act, who can reverse it?

Isa. 43:12-13, NIV

Prayer

Thank you, Lord, for the assurance that the
past is settled and the present and future
are in your hands. Amen.

Praise

O sing to the Lord a new song . . . ,
    all the earth!
For great is the Lord,
    and greatly to be praised;
Ps. 96:1, 4, RSV

Proposal

Do not forget to do good and to share with others, for with such sacrifices God is pleased.
Heb. 13:16, NIV

Practice

Today I'll ask the Lord to fill me with love and generosity in spite of my inclination toward selfishness.

Promise

Nothing will ever be able to separate us from the love of God demonstrated by our Lord Jesus Christ when he died for us.
Rom. 8:39, TLB

Prayer

Thank you, Lord, for the unforgettable lesson on love you taught from the cross. Amen.

October 10

Praise

I will sing a new song unto thee, O God:
> upon a psaltery and an instrument
>> of ten strings
> will I sing praises unto thee.

Ps. 144:9, KJV

Proposal

Let us not grow weary in well-doing, for in
due season we shall reap, if we do not lose
heart.

Gal. 6:9, RSV

Practice

If I feel myself sinking into a negative mood
today, I'll reverse the slide by praising God
and counting my blessings.

Promise

The Lord is righteous
> and loves good deeds;
> those who do them will live in his presence.

Ps. 11:7, TEV

Prayer

Thank you, Lord, for the challenges, responsibilities, and rewards which pack my days.
Amen.

October 11

Praise

Praise be to the Lord from Zion,
    to him who dwells in Jerusalem.
Praise the Lord.

Ps. 135:21, NIV

Proposal

Above all, my beloved, do not swear, either
by heaven or by earth or by any other oath,
but let your "Yes" be yes and your "No" be
no, so that you may not fall under condemnation.

Jas. 5:12, NRSV

Practice

Today I'll say what I mean and do what I
say.

Promise

This God—his way is perfect;
    the promise of the Lord proves true;
he is a shield for all those
    who take refuge in him.

2 Sam. 22:31, RSV

Prayer

Thank you, Lord, for shielding me when I
acknowledge my weaknesses. Amen.

Praise

I will pay my vows to the Lord
   in the presence of all his people,
in the courts of the house of the Lord,
   in your midst, O Jerusalem.
Praise the Lord!

Ps. 116:18-19, RSV

Proposal

Prepare your minds for action; discipline
yourselves; set all your hope on the grace
that Jesus Christ will bring you when he is
revealed.

1 Pet. 1:13, NRSV

Practice

Today I'll ask the Holy Spirit to control my
desires, impulses, and passions.

Promise

[God] hears us whenever we ask him; and
since we know this is true, we know also
that he gives us what we ask from him.

1 John 5:15, TEV

Prayer

Thank you, Lord, for the power available to
me through prayer. Amen.

October 13

Praise

Sing to the Lord a new song,
for he has done marvelous things. . . .
Let the rivers clap their hands,
let the mountains sing together for joy;
let them sing before the Lord.

Ps. 98:1, 8, NIV

Proposal

Never be lacking in zeal, but keep your
spiritual fervor, serving the Lord.

Rom. 12:11, NIV

Practice

Today I'll guard against complacency by
spending time with the Lord and meditating on the wisdom in this book.

Promise

Whatever you ask in my name, I will do it,
that the Father may be glorified in the Son.

John 14:13, RSV

Prayer

Thank you, Lord, for uplifting me when I'm
physically tired and emotionally drained.
Amen.

October 14

Praise

As long as I live I will praise the Lord;
   I will sing psalms to my God
      all my life long.

Ps. 146:2, NEB

Proposal

My beloved, be steadfast, immovable,
always excelling in the work of the Lord,
because you know that in the Lord your
labor is not in vain.

1 Cor. 15:58, NRSV

Practice

Today I'll shape life to my Spirit-guided
preferences by using the power God has
made available to control my thoughts.

Promise

[The Lord] will not let your foot slip—
   he who watches over you . . .
      will neither slumber nor sleep.

Ps. 121:3-4, NIV

Prayer

Thank you, Lord, for giving me inner
security when I spend time with you. Amen.

October 15

Praise

Hallelujah! Yes, let his people praise him
as they stand in his Temple courts.
Praise the Lord because he is so good;
sing to his wonderful name.

Ps. 135:1-3, TLB

Proposal

As the body without the spirit is dead,
so faith without deeds is dead.

Jas. 2:26, NIV

Practice

Today I'll cooperate with the inevitable,
maintain a proper perspective, and rise
above unexpected inconveniences.

Promise

The Lord is still in his holy temple;
he still rules from heaven.
He closely watches everything
that happens here on earth.

Ps. 11:4, TLB

Prayer

Thank you, Lord, for revealing your will and
lighting my path each day. Amen.

October 16

Praise

Sing a new song to the Lord;
    praise him in the assembly
        of his faithful people!

Ps. 149:1, TEV

Proposal

My children, our love is not to be just words
or mere talk, but something real and active.

1 John 3:18, JB

Practice

Today I'll give a smile and show kindness to
everyone who crosses my path.

Promise

Who shall ascend the hill of the Lord? . . .
Those who have clean hands
    and pure hearts,
  who do not lift up their souls
    to what is false,
  and do not swear deceitfully.
They will receive blessing from the Lord.

Ps. 24:3-5, NRSV

Prayer

Thank you, Lord, for letting your real world
warn me from too much fantasy. Amen.

Praise

I will sing to the Lord,
    for he is highly exalted. . . .
He is my God, and I will praise him,
    my father's God, and I will exalt him.

Exod. 15:1-2, NIV

Proposal

Do not lie to one another, seeing that you have put off the old nature with its practices.

Col. 3:9, RSV

Practice

Today, being keenly aware of my old nature, I'll resolve anew to depend upon God rather than myself.

Promise

O fear the Lord, you his holy ones,
    for those who fear him have no want.

Ps. 34:9, NRSV

Prayer

Thank you, Lord, for the serenity to accept the things I cannot change. Amen.

October 18

Praise

All praise the Lord together. . . .
His glory is far greater
  than all of earth and heaven. . . .
Hallelujah! Yes, praise the Lord!

Ps. 148:13-14, TLB

Proposal

I tell you, on the day of judgment you will
have to give an account for every careless
word you utter.

Matt. 12:36, NRSV

Practice

Today I'll surrender to the Lord and use his
Spirit's power to discipline my speech.

Promise

All the ways of the Lord are loving
    and faithful
  for those who keep
    the demands of his covenant.

Ps. 25:10, NIV

Prayer

Thank you, Lord, for enabling me to trans-
cend my own limitations by the power of
your Spirit. Amen.

Praise

Praise [the Lord], all his angels,
all the armies of heaven.
Praise him, sun and moon,
and all you twinkling stars.
Praise him, skies above.

Ps. 148:2-4, TLB

Proposal

If you really keep the royal law found in
Scripture, "Love your neighbor as yourself,"
you are doing right.

Jas. 2:8, NIV

Practice

Today I'll develop self-esteem by reinforc-
ing positive qualities in others.

Promise

God will redeem my soul
from the power of the grave.

Ps. 49:15, NKJB

Prayer

Thank you, Lord, for the gift of life, the gift
of eternal life, and the privilege of fellow-
shiping with you each day. Amen.

October 20

Praise

Oh, come, let us sing to the Lord!
　Give a joyous shout in honor
　　of the Rock of our salvation!
Come before him with thankful hearts.
　Let us sing him psalms of praise.

Ps. 95:1-2, TLB

Proposal

Do not let sin control your puny body any
longer; do not give in to its sinful desires.

Rom. 6:12, TLB

Practice

Today I'll deceive or exploit no one under
any circumstances.

Promise

Many sorrows come to the wicked,
　but abiding love surrounds
　　those who trust in the Lord.

Ps. 32:10, TLB

Prayer

Thank you, Lord, for liberating me from
depending on the approval of others.
Amen.

Praise

Sing to the Lord, you saints of his;
    praise his holy name.

Ps. 30:4, NIV

Proposal

Be angry but do not sin;
    do not let the sun go down on your anger.

Eph. 4:26, RSV

Practice

If negative emotions, undisciplined impulses, or bursts of anger thrust themselves upon me today, I'll immediately seek the Lord's assistance.

Promise

I will give you the keys of the kingdom of heaven; whatever you bind on earth will be bound in heaven, and whatever you loose on earth will be loosed in heaven.

Matt. 16:19, NIV

Prayer

Thank you, Lord, for the power of Spirit-filled, Christ-centered prayer. Amen.

October 22

Praise

Praise the Lord.
How good it is to sing praises to our God,
   how pleasant and fitting to praise him!

Ps. 147:1, NIV

Proposal

Beloved, do not believe every spirit, but test
the spirits to see whether they are of God;
for many false prophets have gone out into
the world.

1 John 4:1, RSV

Practice

Today I'll confront the discord in my life by
applying the insight I've received through
spiritual revelation.

Promise

[The Lord] guides the humble in what is
right and teaches them his way.

Ps. 25:9, NIV

Prayer

Thank you, Lord, for leading me in the way
of righteousness and increasing my inner
security. Amen.

October 23

Praise

O praise the Lord, all ye nations:
    praise him, all ye people. . . .
Praise ye the Lord.

Ps. 117:1-2, KJV

Proposal

Take up the whole armor of God, so that
you may be able to withstand on that evil
day, and having done everything, to stand
firm.

Eph. 6:13, NRSV

Practice

Today I'll rely upon the Lord for security,
strength, and comfort.

Promise

You love righteousness
    and hate wickedness;
therefore God, your God, has set you
    above your companions
    by anointing you with the oil of joy.

Ps. 45:7, NIV

Prayer

Thank you, Lord, for enabling me to be at
peace with myself and with others. Amen.

October 24

Praise

Let them praise the name of the Lord:
>   for his name alone is exalted;
>   his glory is above the earth and heaven.

Ps. 148:13, RSV

Proposal

Humble yourselves before the Lord,
>   and he will lift you up.

Jas. 4:10, NIV

Practice

Today I'll search the innermost recesses of my being and see myself as I really am, a sinner in need of forgiveness and grace.

Promise

Know that the Lord has set apart
>   the godly for himself;
>   the Lord will hear when I call to him.

Ps. 4:3, NIV

Prayer

Thank you, Lord, for the assurance that you will give more strength to me for those difficult situations certain to come along. Amen.

October 25

Praise

Praise him with the cymbals,
    yes, loud clanging cymbals.
Let everything alive
    give praises to the Lord!

Ps. 150:5-6, TLB

Proposal

Do not put out the Spirit's fire; do not treat
prophecies with contempt. Test everything.
Hold on to the good. Avoid every kind
of evil.

1 Thess. 5:19-22, NIV

Practice

Today I'll acknowledge God's authority,
submit to his will, and yield to his Spirit.

Promise

Now therefore hearken unto me,
    O ye children:
for blessed are they that keep my ways.

Prov. 8:32, KJV

Prayer

Thank you, Lord, for enabling me to deal
with my failings and develop my character
constructively. Amen.

October 26

Praise

Oh that [everyone] would praise the Lord
for his goodness,
    and for his wonderful works.

Ps. 107:8, KJV

Proposal

Let your light shine before others, so that
they may see your good deeds and give
glory to your Father in heaven.

Matt. 5:16, NRSV

Practice

Today I refuse to lower my values in the
pursuit of any endeavor, regardless of how
noble.

Promise

Who are they that fear the Lord?
    He will teach them the way that
        they should choose.

Ps. 25:12, NRSV

Prayer

Thank you, Lord, for the enormous sense of
satisfaction you give me when I conform to
your will. Amen.

October 27

Praise

I will praise you, my God and King,
and bless your name each day and forever.

Ps. 145:1, TLB

Proposal

Whoever says, "I have come to know
[God]," but does not obey his commandments, is a liar, and in such a person the
truth does not exist.

1 John 2:4, NRSV

Practice

I refuse to turn away from the Lord during
periods of distress. Today I'll face each
situation with courage, faith, and
determination.

Promise

Keep my commands, . . . for they will
prolong your life many years and bring you
prosperity.

Prov. 3:1-2, NIV

Prayer

Thank you, Lord, for the valuable lessons of
life that usually result after periods of
intense inner struggle. Amen.

Praise

I will praise God's name in song
   and glorify him with thanksgiving.

Ps. 69:30, NIV

Proposal

You must get rid of all such things—anger,
wrath, malice, slander, and abusive
language from your mouth.

Col. 3:8, NRSV

Practice

Today I'll maintain good interpersonal
relationships by listening before speaking
and being especially sensitive to the other
person's point of view.

Promise

The meek shall possess the land,
   and delight themselves in
      abundant prosperity.

Ps. 37:11, RSV

Prayer

Thank you, Lord, for enabling me to
neutralize negative inner forces that
attempt to control me. Amen.

Praise

I will praise your name continually [Lord],
 fulfilling my vow of praising you each day.

Ps. 61:8, TLB

Proposal

Do not think of yourself more highly than
you should. Instead, be modest in your
thinking.

Rom. 12:3, TEV

Practice

Today I'll take credit for legitimate
accomplishments, but under no circumstances will I pretend to be something I'm
not.

Promise

I sought the Lord, and he answered me;
 he delivered me from all my fears.

Ps. 34:4, NIV

Prayer

Thank you, Lord, for your unconditional
love which impels me to be more effective
in ongoing relationships. Amen.

October 30

Praise

I will give thanks unto thee, O Lord,
>among the heathen,
>and I will sing praises unto thy name.

2 Sam. 22:50, KJV

Proposal

Be joyful always; pray continually; give
thanks in all circumstances, for this is God's
will for you in Christ Jesus.

1 Thess. 5:16-18, NIV

Practice

Today I'll remember to pray, praise God,
and give thanks in all things.

Promise

Even strong young lions
>sometimes go hungry,
>but those of us who reverence the Lord
>will never lack any good thing.

Ps. 34:10, TLB

Prayer

Thank you, Lord, for enabling me to accept
the past and to have confidence in the
future under your rule. Amen.

Praise

Sing to God, O kingdoms of the earth,
   sing praise to the Lord. *Selah.*

Ps. 68:32, NIV

Proposal

You are the salt of the earth. But if the salt loses its saltiness, how can it be made salty again?

Matt. 5:13, NIV

Practice

Today I refuse to place limitations upon myself by listening to those who would tell me all the things I cannot do.

Promise

[God's servant] was wounded for our
      transgressions,
   he was bruised for our iniquities.

Isa. 53:5, RSV

Prayer

Thank you, Lord Jesus, for submitting to excruciating mental and physical torture when you died for me. Amen.

November 1

Praise
The shepherds returned, glorifying and praising God for all the things they had heard and seen.

Luke 2:20, NIV

Proposal
Show by your good life that your works are done with gentleness born of wisdom. . . . Do not be boastful and false to the truth.

Jas. 3:13-14, NRSV

Practice
Today I'll humbly ask the Lord for power to overcome my shortcomings, starting with the most conspicuous.

Promise
God is our refuge and strength,
a tested help in times of trouble.

Ps. 46:1, TLB

Prayer
Thank you, Lord, for the sense of harmony, inner strength, and deep satisfaction that come from living for you. Amen.

Praise

I will love thee, O Lord, my strength. . . .
  I will call upon the Lord,
    who is worthy to be praised.

Ps. 18:1, 3, KJV

Proposal

Do not be worried about the food and drink
you need in order to stay alive, or about
clothes for your body.

Matt. 6:25, TEV

Practice

Today I refuse to worship idols such as
pleasure, money, or power.

Promise

Our steps are made firm by the Lord,
  when he delights in our way;
though we stumble, we shall not
    fall headlong,
  for the Lord holds us by the hand.

Ps. 37:23-24, NRSV

Prayer

Thank you, Lord, for enabling me to fulfill
legitimate needs, such as love, security, and
acceptance. Amen.

November 3

Praise

Praise the Lord. . . .
Praise him for his acts of power;
   praise him for his surpassing greatness.

Ps. 150:1-2, NIV

Proposal

The Scriptures say, "Worship only the Lord
God. Obey only him."

Matt. 4:10, TLB

Practice

Today I'll willingly place myself in God's
hands to transform me and strengthen my
character.

Promise

Those who love me,
   I, [the Lord,] will deliver;
   I will protect those who know my name.
When they call to me, I will answer them;
   I will be with them in trouble,
   I will rescue them and honor them.

Ps. 91:14-15, NRSV

Prayer

Thank you, Lord, for calming my anxieties
and neutralizing my fears. Amen.

Praise

O God, my heart is ready to praise you!
    I will sing and rejoice before you. . . .
I will praise you everywhere
    around the world, in every nation.

Ps. 108:1, 3, TLB

Proposal

Love your enemies and pray for those who
persecute you,

Matt. 5:44, NIV

Practice

Today I'll make every effort to manifest the
love of Christ toward those who dislike me.

Promise

To be carnally minded is death,
    but to be spiritually minded
        is life and peace.

Rom. 8:6, NKJB

Prayer

Thank you, Lord, for freeing me from sin,
self-preoccupation, and dependence on
other people's approval. Amen.

November 5

Praise

And the twenty-four elders, who were seated on their thrones before God, fell on their faces and worshiped God, saying:

"We give thanks to you,
Lord God Almighty."

Rev. 11:16-17, NIV

Proposal

Give thanks in all circumstances; for this is the will of God in Christ Jesus for you.

1 Thess. 5:18, RSV

Practice

Today I'll seek intimate contact and meaningful fellowship with God through prayer and meditation.

Promise

How awesome is God as he comes
from his sanctuary—the God of Israel!
He gives strength and power to his people.

Ps. 68:35, TEV

Prayer

Thank you, Lord, for the silent strength of humility when pride nips at me. Amen.

November 6

Praise

Mary said:
"My soul glorifies the Lord
and my spirit rejoices in God my Savior."
Luke 1:46-47, NIV

Proposal

[Jesus said,] "If you refuse to take up your
cross and follow me, you are not worthy of
being mine."
Matt. 10:38, TLB

Practice

Today I'll celebrate my relationship with
God by praising him in every situation.

Promise

The salvation of the righteous
comes from the Lord. . . .
He delivers them from the wicked
and saves them,
because they take refuge in him.
Ps. 37:39-40, NIV

Prayer

Thank you, Lord, for the blessings I enjoy
but often take for granted. Amen.

Praise

I will give thanks in the Great Assembly,
 praise you where the people throng. . . .
Then my tongue will shout your goodness,
 and sing your praises all day long.

Ps. 35:18, 28, JB

Proposal

Peter and the other apostles answered,
 "We must obey God rather than
 any human authority."

Acts 5:29, NRSV

Practice

Today I'll covet God's loving Spirit and
make every effort to be obedient to God.

Promise

[God] shall give his angels charge over thee,
 to keep thee in all thy ways.
They shall bear thee up in their hands,
 lest thou dash thy foot against a stone.

Ps. 91:11-12, KJV

Prayer

Thank you, Father, for revealing your
character through the life of Jesus. Amen.

November 8

Praise

I will praise you among the nations, O Lord;
   I will sing praises to your name.

Ps. 18:49, NIV

Proposal

Do not deceive one another. . . . Do not
defraud your neighbor. . . . Do not seek
revenge or bear a grudge against one of
your people, but love your neighbor as
yourself.

Lev. 19:11, 13, 18, NIV

Practice

Today I'll trust the Lord for courage to
reconcile with others by asking for forgiveness and by extending forgiveness.

Promise

He guards the course of the just
   and protects the way
      of his faithful ones.

Prov. 2:8, NIV

Prayer

Thank you, Lord, for the assurance that you
understand me better than I understand
myself. Amen.

November 9

Praise

I looked and heard the voice of many
angels. . . . In a loud voice they sang:
  "Worthy is the Lamb, who was slain,
    to receive power and wealth
      and wisdom and strength
    and honor and glory and praise!"

Rev. 5:11-12, NIV

Proposal

In everything do to others as you would
have them do to you.

Matt. 7:12, NRSV

Practice

Today I'll help others find what I've found:
love, security, self-worth, and peace
through a personal relationship with God
through Jesus Christ.

Promise

Seek your happiness in the Lord,
  and he will give you your heart's desire.

Ps. 37:4, TEV

Prayer

Thank you, Lord, for your Word, that
nourishes my soul and lifts my spirit. Amen.

Praise

Simeon took [Jesus] in his arms and praised
God, saying . . .

"My eyes have seen your salvation."

Luke 2:28, NIV

Proposal

[Jesus] answered, "It is written,
'One does not live by bread alone,
but by every word that comes
from the mouth of God.' "

Matt. 4:4, NRSV

Practice

Today I'll release to the Lord any destructive
thoughts that would drag me down.

Promise

God blesses those who are kind to the poor.
He helps them out of their troubles. . . .
He nurses them when they are sick,
and soothes their pains and worries.

Ps. 41:1, 3, TLB

Prayer

Thank you, Lord, for your willingness to
bless far above my ability to ask or even
think. Amen.

November 11

Praise

The Lord lives! Praise be to my Rock!
Exalted be God, the Rock, my Savior!

2 Sam. 22:47, NIV

Proposal

Do not be ashamed then of testifying to our
Lord . . . but share in suffering for the
gospel in the power of God.

2 Tim. 1:8, RSV

Practice

Today I'll accept myself as I am, an
imperfect human being who's allowed to
make mistakes.

Promise

The Lord bestows favor and honor;
   no good thing does he withhold
      from those whose walk is blameless.

Ps. 84:11, NIV

Prayer

Thank you, Lord, for enabling me to shift
my focus away from how large the
problems are, so I can see the life-changing
potential of your awesome power. Amen.

Praise

Give thanks to the Lord,
    proclaim his greatness;
    tell the nations what he has done.

1 Chron. 16:8, TEV

Proposal

Say just a simple "Yes, I will" or "No, I won't." Your word is enough. To strengthen your promise with a vow shows that something is wrong.

Matt. 5:37, TLB

Practice

Today I'll be accountable to the Lord, to my family, and to those with whom I'm bonded through Christ.

Promise

Happy are those who consider the poor;
    the Lord delivers them
        in the day of trouble.

Ps. 41:1, NRSV

Prayer

Thank you, Lord, for loving me in spite of seasons when I rebel or am selfish. Amen.

Praise

I will praise you, O Lord,
    among the nations. . . .
Be exalted, O God, above the heavens;
    let your glory be over all the earth.

Ps. 57:9, 11, NIV

Proposal

Don't be afraid of those who can kill only
your bodies—but can't touch your souls!
Fear only God who can destroy both soul
and body in hell.

Matt. 10:28, TLB

Practice

Today I'll be faithful to the Lord while trusting in him for success in right living.

Promise

The salvation of the righteous
    comes from the Lord;
    he is their stronghold in time of trouble.

Ps. 37:39, NIV

Prayer

Thank you, Lord, for your loving kindness
to such an undeserving person as myself.
Amen.

November 14

Praise

Thou has saved us from our enemies,
    and hast put them to shame that hated us.
In God we boast all the day long,
    and praise thy name for ever. Selah.

Ps. 44:7-8, KJV

Proposal

God is Spirit: and those who worship him
must worship in spirit and truth.

John 4:24, NRSV

Practice

Today I'll worship and praise the Lord with
undivided attention in the sanctuary
of my soul.

Promise

For this God is our God for ever and ever;
    he will be our guide even to the end.

Ps. 48:14, NIV

Prayer

Thank you, Lord, for your patience, forgiving nature, and infinite grace. Amen.

November 15

Praise

Extol the Lord our God,
    and worship at his holy mountain;
        for the Lord our God is holy!

Ps. 99:9, RSV

Proposal

Let us hold fast the confession of our hope
without wavering, for [God] who promised
is faithful.

Heb. 10:23, RSV

Practice

Today I'll surrender my life as completely as
possible to the Holy Spirit's control and
accept the Spirit's direction regardless of
where it leads.

Promise

Evening, morning and noon
    I cry out in distress,
    and [the Lord] hears my voice.

Ps. 55:17, NIV

Prayer

Thank you, Lord, for the gift of the Holy
Spirit, who infuses me with the fruit of love,
peace, joy, patience, and self-control. Amen.

November 16

Praise

When all the Israelites saw the fire coming down and the glory of the Lord above the temple . . . they worshiped and gave thanks to the Lord.

2 Chron. 7:3, NIV

Proposal

It is God's will that by doing right you should silence the ignorance of the foolish.

1 Pet. 2:15, NRSV

Practice

Today I'll search the dark recesses of my mind for any unresolved sin that needs to be confessed.

Promise

The righteous cry, and the Lord heareth,
 and delivereth them out of
  all their troubles.

Ps. 34:17, KJV

Prayer

Thank you, Lord, for renewal in moments of silence when I'm dizzy from being busy in a hectic world. Amen.

November 17

Praise

I will be glad, yes, filled with joy
    because of you.
I will sing your praises,
    O Lord God above all gods.

Ps. 9:2, TLB

Proposal

Where there is jealousy and selfishness,
there is also disorder and every kind of evil.

Jas. 3:16, TEV

Practice

Today I'll enhance my own spiritual growth
by sharing my faith and encouraging
others.

Promise

With all his abundant wealth through Christ
Jesus, my God will supply all your needs.

Phil. 4:19, TEV

Prayer

Thank you, Lord, for the privilege of being
your servant, living by faith, and experienc-
ing countless blessings. Amen.

Praise

O come, let us worship and bow down. . . .
For he is our God,
  and we are the people of his pasture,
    and the sheep of his hand.

Ps. 95:6-7, RSV

Proposal

Pursue peace with everyone, and the holiness without which no one will see the Lord.

Heb. 12:14, NRSV

Practice

Today I'll look at difficult relationships from the perspective of my responsibility, regardless of the problem.

Promise

Love and faithfulness . . . will win [for you] favor and a good name in the sight of God.

Prov. 3:3-4, NIV

Prayer

Thank you, Lord Jesus, for the success I've enjoyed solely due to my relationship with you. Amen.

November 19

Praise

I will extol you, my God and King,
  and bless your name forever and ever.
Every day I will bless you,
  and praise your name forever and ever.

Ps. 145:1-2, KJV

Proposal

When [people] talk too much,
  sin is never far away;
  common sense holds its tongue.

Prov. 10:19, NEB

Practice

Today I'll surrender my will to the Holy
Spirit, with the assurance that the Spirit will
enable me to control my tongue.

Promise

[God] will keep you strong to the end, so
that you will be blameless on the day of our
Lord Jesus Christ.

1 Cor. 1:8, NIV

Prayer

Thank you, Lord, for forgiving my errant
past and being the source of my healthy
self-esteem. Amen.

Praise

How everyone throughout the earth
  will praise the Lord! . . .
Praise God, O world!
  May all the peoples of the earth
    give thanks to you.

Ps. 67:3, 5, TLB

Proposal

Love your enemies, do good to them, and
lend to them without expecting to get anything back.

Luke 6:35, NIV

Practice

Today I'll draw closer to the Lord by forgiving those who have harmed me.

Promise

[Jesus said,] "In the world you face persecu-
tion. But take courage; I have conquered
the world!"

John 16:33, NRSV

Prayer

Thank you, Lord, for enabling me to deal
creatively with destructive thoughts that
accompany angry or fearful temper. Amen.

November 21

Praise

We your people, the sheep of your pasture,
    will thank you forever and forever,
    praising your greatness
        from generation to generation.

Ps. 79:13, TLB

Proposal

Keep alert, stand firm in your faith, be
courageous, be strong. Let all that you do be
done in love.

1 Cor. 16:13 14, NRSV

Practice

Today I'll acknowledge my weaknesses and
depend on the presence of the Holy Spirit
for strength.

Promise

Sin shall not be your master, because you
are not under law, but under grace.

Rom. 6:14, NIV

Prayer

Thank you, Lord, for *not* requiring me to
redeem myself through self-achievement,
self-sacrifice, or self-fulfillment. Amen.

Praise

In a great antiphonal chorus they sang,
   "Holy, holy, holy is the Lord of Hosts;
   the whole earth is filled with his glory."

Isa. 6:3, TLB

Proposal

Follow the way of love and eagerly desire
spiritual gifts, especially the gift of
prophecy.

1 Cor. 14:1, NIV

Practice

Today I'll attempt to follow Jesus' example,
showing compassion for the downtrodden.

Promise

You who live in the shelter
      of the Most High,
   who abide in the shadow of the Almighty,
will say to the Lord,
   "My refuge and my fortress;
      my God, in whom I trust."

Ps. 91:1-2, NIV

Prayer

Thank you, Lord, for never leaving me to
face the burdens of life alone. Amen.

Praise

Sing to the Lord, all the earth.
    Tell of his salvation from day to day.
Declare his glory among the nations,
    his marvelous works among all
        the peoples.

1 Chron. 16:23-24, NRSV

Proposal

Never let yourself think that you are wiser
than you are; simply obey the Lord and
refuse to do wrong.

Prov. 3:7, TEV

Practice

Today I'll come to the Lord like a little child,
open, trusting, and willing to be used.

Promise

[Jesus said,] "Peace I bequeath to you, my
own peace I give you, a peace the world
cannot give, this is my gift to you."

John 14:27, JB

Prayer

Thank you, Lord, for inner peace and
security that allows me to think clearly and
establish realistic goals. Amen.

November 24

Praise

The Lord lives! Praise be to my Rock!
Exalted be God my Savior! . . .
He is the God . . .
who saves me from my enemies.
I will sing praises to your name.

Ps. 18:46-49, NIV

Proposal

Let [God] have all your worries and cares,
for he is always thinking about you and
watching everything that concerns you.

1 Pet. 5:7, TLB

Practice

Today I'll exercise my faith by focusing on
possibilities rather than problems.

Promise

The Lord is near to those
who are discouraged;
he saves those who have lost all hope.

Ps. 34:18, TEV

Prayer

Thank you, Lord, for not abandoning me
when I revert to old character habits that get
me into trouble. Amen.

Praise

Lord, who will not fear
and glorify your name?
For you alone are holy.
All nations will come
and worship before you,
for your judgments have been revealed.

Rev. 14:4, NRSV

Proposal

Pride leads to arguments;
be humble, take advice and become wise.

Prov. 13:10, TLB

Practice

Today I'll confess my sins and receive
forgiveness and cleansing.

Promise

The Lord will guide you continually,
and satisfy you with all good things,
and keep you healthy too.

Isa. 58:11, TLB

Prayer

Thank you, Lord, for never failing to reward
me when I step out in faith. Amen.

Praise

Sing out your praises to our God, our King.
Yes, sing your highest praises to our King,
the King of all the earth.

Ps. 47:6-7, TLB

Proposal

Be strong and courageous.
Do not be afraid or discouraged.

1 Chron. 22:13, NIV

Practice

Today I'll acknowledge my weaknesses and
look to the Lord for the strength to overcome any difficulty.

Promise

Humility and the fear of the Lord
bring wealth and honor and life.

Prov. 22:4, NIV

Prayer

Thank you, Lord, for the beauty of creation,
the fragrance of flowers, the singing of
birds, the warmth of the sun, and the savor
of good food. Amen.

Praise

"To him who sits on the throne
and to the Lamb,
be praise and honor, glory and might,
forever and ever!"

Rev. 5:13, TEV

Proposal

Do not worship any other gods or . . . serve them.

2 Kings 17:35, NIV

Practice

Today I'll follow the Lord by drawing on his strength, aligning my thoughts with his Word, and dedicating my efforts to serving him.

Promise

Though heart and body fail,
yet God is my possession for ever.

Ps. 73:26, NEB

Prayer

Thank you, Lord, for holy dreams and visions that keep my imagination occupied and stimulated. Amen.

Praise

Praise the Lord! . . .
Praise his name with dancing;
   play drums and harps in praise of him.

Ps. 149:1, 3, TEV

Proposal

Be sure . . . you are never spiteful, or deceitful, or hypocritical, or envious and critical of each other.

1 Pet. 2:1, JB

Practice

Today I'll express my love for the Lord by exercising self-restraint and placing the rights of others ahead of my own.

Promise

[Jesus said,] "The Advocate, the Holy Spirit, whom the Father will send in my name, will teach you everything."

John 14:26, NRSV

Prayer

Thank you, Lord, for the gift of faith that overcomes the two biggest fears in the world, the fear of dying and the fear of living. Amen.

November 29

Praise

Alleluia!
Give thanks to Yahweh, call his name aloud,
    proclaim his deeds to the peoples! . . .
Glory in his holy name,
    let the hearts that seek Yahweh rejoice!

Ps. 105:1, 3, JB

Proposal

Do not let this happy trust in the Lord die
away, no matter what happens.

Heb. 10:35, TLB

Practice

Today I'll acknowledge my human
weaknesses and rely upon the Spirit of God
for victory, even in rough circumstances.

Promise

I am like a green olive tree
    in the house of God.
I trust in the steadfast love of God
    forever and ever.

Ps. 52:8, NRSV

Prayer

Thank you, Lord, for guiding me through
the storms of life. Amen.

Praise

O Lord, God of Israel, there is no God like you in heaven or on earth—you who keep your covenant of love with your servants who continue wholeheartedly in your way.

2 Chron. 6:14, NIV

Proposal

Do not rejoice when your enemies fall,
    and do not let your heart be glad
        when they stumble.

Prov. 24:17, NRSV

Practice

Today I'll suspend judgment toward others and forgive those who have offended me.

Promise

The Lord redeems the life of his servants;
    none of those who take refuge in him
        will be condemned.

Ps. 34:22, NRSV

Prayer

Thank you, Lord, for the fellowship, secure thoughts, and pleasurable anticipations your presence gives me. Amen.

December 1

Praise

I thank you, Yahweh, with all my heart;
    I recite your marvels one by one,
I rejoice and exult in you,
    I sing praise to your name, Most High.

Ps. 9:1-2, JB

Proposal

Endure trials for the sake of discipline. God is treating you as children; for what child is there whom a parent does not discipline?

Heb. 12:7, NRSV

Practice

Today I'll resist the temptation to give in to temper or allow my attitude to be determined by trifles beyond my control.

Promise

So it is with the resurrection of the dead. What is sown is perishable, what is raised is imperishable. . . . If there is a physical body, there is also a spiritual body.

1 Cor. 15:42, 44, NRSV

Prayer

Thank you, Lord, for the sheer joy of sleep when I'm terribly tired. Amen.

December 2

Praise

"Blessed be God Most High,
    who has delivered your enemies
        into your hand!"
And Abram gave [Melchizedek, priest of
God Most High,] one tenth of everything.

Gen. 14:19-20, NRSV

Proposal

Whoever wants to enjoy life
    and wishes to see good times,
must keep from speaking evil
    and stop telling lies.

1 Pet. 3:10, TEV

Practice

Today I'll remain focused on who I am and
the direction God wants for me.

Promise

You will reveal the path of life to me . . . and
    at your right hand everlasting pleasures.

Ps. 16:11, JB

Prayer

Thank you, Lord, for the sense of well-being
you supply from firsthand experience and
communion with you. Amen.

December 3

Praise

Sing for joy to the Lord, all the earth;
   praise him with songs and shouts of joy!

Ps. 98:4, TEV

Proposal

Beloved, I urge you as aliens and exiles to
abstain from the desires of the flesh that
wage war against the soul.

1 Pet. 2:11, NRSV

Practice

Today I'll thoroughly evaluate my life,
accept the truth about myself, and guard
against hypocrisy.

Promise

[Jesus said,] "They who have my commandments and keep them are those who love
me; and those who love me will be loved by
my Father, and I will love them and reveal
myself to them."

John 14:21, JB

Prayer

Thank you, Lord, for showing me your kingdom when I come before you with a humble heart. Amen.

December 4

Praise

Sing your praise accompanied by
    music from the harp. . . .
Let the sea in all its vastness
    roar with praise! . . . Shout,
"Glory to the Lord."

Ps. 98:5, 7, TLB

Proposal

The commandments . . . "Do not covet,"
and whatever other commandment there
may be, are summed up in this one rule:
"Love your neighbor as yourself."

Rom. 13:9, NIV

Practice

I refuse to stray from trusting God through
either inattention or disobedience.

Promise

You shall therefore be careful to do the
commandment. . . . And the Lord will take
away from you all sickness.

Deut. 7:11, 15, RSV

Prayer

Thank you, Lord, for being patient with me
when I question your will. Amen.

December 5

Praise

Because of [the Lord's] great power
    he rules forever.
He watches every movement of the nations.
. . . Let everyone bless God
        and sing his praises.

Ps. 66:7-8, TLB

Proposal

Let everyone see that you are unselfish and
considerate in all you do.

Phil. 4:5, TLB

Practice

Today I'll serve the Lord with gladness by
expressing a gentle, caring attitude toward
others.

Promise

The Lord is a stronghold for the oppressed,
    a stronghold in times of trouble.

Ps. 9:9, NRSV

Prayer

Thank you, Lord, for your grace, that is wide
enough and deep enough to include even
me, a weak and sinful human being. Amen.

December 6

Praise
My tongue will speak of your righteousness,
[O Lord,] and of your praises all day long.
Ps. 35:28, NIV

Proposal
Avoid anything in your everyday lives that
would be unworthy of the gospel of Christ.
Phil. 1:27, JB

Practice
Today I refuse to allow cynicism or skep-
ticism to corrode my spirit or give rise to
negative thinking.

Promise
[Jesus said,] "These things have I spoken
unto you, that my joy might remain in you,
and that your joy might be full."
John 15:11, KJV

Prayer
Thank you, Lord, for transforming my
previously aimless existence into an orga-
nized, meaningful, and purposeful life.
Amen.

Praise

Sing to the Lord; praise the Lord!
For he has delivered the life of the needy
from the hand of evildoers.

Jer. 20:13, RSV

Proposal

Fear God and give him glory, because the
hour of his judgment has come. Worship
him who made the heavens, the earth, the
sea and the springs of water.

Rev. 14:7, NIV

Practice

Today I'll take a few minutes during periods
of stress to reflect upon God's wonderful
creation and his reign over it.

Promise

He stores up sound wisdom for the upright;
[the Lord] is a shield to those
who walk blamelessly.

Prov. 2:7, NRSV

Prayer

Thank you, Lord, for aiding my accomplishments and reminding me that without you I
can do nothing of lasting value. Amen.

December 8

Praise

Bless Yahweh, my soul,
    bless his holy name, all that is in me!
Bless Yahweh, my soul,
    and remember all his kindnesses.

Ps. 103:1-2, JB

Proposal

Most important of all, continue to show
deep love for each other, for love makes up
for many of your faults.

1 Pet. 4:8, TLB

Practice

Today I'll face every task with the confident
expectation of success because of Christ.

Promise

[The Lord] will keep in perfect peace
    all those who trust in him,
    whose thoughts turn often to the Lord!

Isa. 26:3, TLB

Prayer

Thank you, Lord, for being my hiding place
and surrounding me with steadfast love.
Amen.

December 9

Praise

[The Lord] is my strength,
   my shield from every danger. . . .
Joy rises in my heart
   until I burst out in songs of praise to him.

Ps. 28:7, TLB

Proposal

Honor everyone. Love the family of
believers. Fear God. Honor the emperor.

1 Pet. 2:17, NRSV

Practice

Today I'll enjoy a healthy attitude toward
others by praying for their well-being.

Promise

By [the Lord's] divine power, he has given
us all the things that we need for life and for
true devotion, bringing us to know God
himself.

2 Pet. 1:3, JB

Prayer

Thank you, Lord, for loving me unconditionally in spite of myself. Amen.

December 10

Praise

All you that are righteous,
    shout for joy for what the Lord has done;
praise him, all you that obey him.

Ps. 33:1, TEV

Proposal

Do not let any unwholesome talk come out
of your mouths, but only what is helpful for
building others up according to their needs,
that it may benefit those who listen.

Eph. 4:29, NIV

Practice

Today I'll take every opportunity to say
good things about people who dislike me.

Promise

[Jesus said,] "No, I will not abandon you or
leave you as orphans in the storm—I will
come to you."

John 14:18, TLB

Prayer

Thank you, Lord, for carrying me when the
load becomes too heavy. Amen.

December 11

Praise

Blessed be Jehovah God, the God of Israel,
   who only does wonderful things.
Blessed be his glorious name forever!
   Let the whole earth be filled with his glory.
Amen, and amen!

Ps. 72:18-19, TLB

Proposal

Don't worry about anything, but in all your
prayers ask God for what you need, always
asking him with a thankful heart.

Phil. 4:6, TEV

Practice

Today I'll look at every problem as contain-
ing a lesson to be learned.

Promise

You can get anything—*anything* you ask for
in prayer—if you believe.

Matt. 21:22, TLB

Prayer

Thank you, Lord, for the sense of
accomplishment that results from exercising my faith. Amen.

December 12

Praise
Gladly I bring my sacrifices to you;
I will praise your name, O Lord,
for it is good.

Ps. 54:6, TLB

Proposal
Do your best to present yourself to God as
one approved by him, a worker who has no
need to be ashamed, rightly explaining the
word of truth.

2 Tim. 2:15, NRSV

Practice
Today I'll relinquish self-will, dependencies,
and excessive ambitions to the Lord.

Promise
When you go through deep waters
and great trouble,
I will be with you.

Isa. 43:2, TLB

Prayer
Thank you, Lord, for coming to my
assistance when I'm my own worst enemy.
Amen.

December 13

Praise

Sing to the Lord because of the great things
    he has done.
    Let the whole world hear the news.
Let everyone who lives in Zion
    shout and sing!

Isa. 12:5-6, TEV

Proposal

Do not deceive yourselves. . . . You should
become fools so that you may become
wise.

1 Cor. 3:18, NRSV

Practice

Today I refuse to rely on willpower to keep
me focused on God's will. Instead, I'll
depend on the power of the Holy Spirit.

Promise

The Lord will keep your going out
    and your coming in
from this time on and forevermore.

Ps. 121:8, NRSV

Prayer

Thank you, Lord, for being my protector
and ultimate source of comfort. Amen.

December 14

Praise

Rejoice in the Lord
>and be glad, you righteous;
>sing, all you who are upright in heart!

Ps. 32:11, NIV

Proposal

We destroy arguments and every proud obstacle raised up against the knowledge of God, and we take every thought captive to obey Christ.

2 Cor. 10:4-5, NRSV

Practice

I refuse to lapse into negative thinking or brood over situations over which I have no control.

Promise

Even to your old age and gray hairs . . .
>I, [the Lord,] have made you
>and I will carry you;
I will sustain you and I will rescue you.

Isa. 46:4, NIV

Prayer

Thank you, Lord, for satisfying my needs and helping me grow old gracefully. Amen.

December 15

Praise

"Blessed be Jehovah, God of Israel,
    Forever and forevermore."
And all the people shouted "Amen!"
    and praised the Lord.

1 Chron. 16:36, TLB

Proposal

Praise the Lord, O my soul!
I will praise the Lord as long as I live;
I will sing praises to my God all my life long.

Ps. 146:1-2, NRSV

Practice

Today I'll stand on the promises of Scripture
and praise the Lord in all situations.

Promise

Cast your cares on the Lord
    and he will sustain you;
        he will never let the righteous fall.

Ps. 55:22, NIV

Prayer

Thank you, Lord, for pricking my conscience when I am tempted to go astray.
Amen.

December 16

Praise

How great is the Lord!
How much we should praise him.

Ps. 48:1, TLB

Proposal

We who are strong ought to put up with the failings of the weak, and not to please ourselves. Each of us must please our neighbor for the good purpose of building up the neighbor.

Rom: 15:1-2, NRSV

Practice

Today I'll concentrate more on what needs to be changed in me rather than what needs to be changed in the world.

Promise

[Wisdom calls out,]
"I love those who love me,
and those who seek me find me."

Prov. 8:17, NIV

Prayer

Lord, I give you thanks in advance for the strength that will be waiting for me alongside every load I must carry. Amen.

December 17

Praise

Praise the Lord, all people on earth,
  praise his glory and might. . . .
Bow down before the Lord
    when he appears in his holiness;
  tremble before him, all the earth!

1 Chron. 16:28-30, TEV

Proposal

Be careful, however, that the exercise of
your freedom does not become a stumbling
block to the weak.

1 Cor. 8:9, NIV

Practice

If I stumble today, I'll learn from failure and
adjust rather than blame others.

Promise

The wicked earn no real gain,
  but those who sow righteousness
    get a true reward.

Prov. 11:18, NRSV

Prayer

Thank you, Lord, for the ability to see
humor in annoying situations. Amen.

December 18

Praise

Alleluia!
Give thanks to Yahweh, for he is good,
his love is everlasting.

Ps. 107:1, JB

Proposal

You know the commandments: "Do not
murder, do not commit adultery, do not
steal, do not give false testimony, do not
defraud, honor your father and mother."

Mark 10:19, NIV

Practice

Instead of rationalizing my shortcomings,
today I'll ask the Lord for strength to overcome them.

Promise

These are all the laws that the Lord your
God commanded me to teach you. . . .
Obey them! Then all will go well with you.

Deut. 6:1, 3, TEV

Prayer

Thank you, Lord, for doing for me what I
could not do for myself. Amen.

December 19

Praise

I thank you, Lord, with all my heart;
  I sing praise to you before the gods.
I face your holy Temple,
  bow down, and praise your name.

Ps. 138:1-2, TEV

Proposal

This is [God's] command: to believe in the
name of his Son, Jesus Christ, and to love
one another as he commanded us.

1 John 3:23, NIV

Practice

Today I'll ask the Holy Spirit to fill my heart
with unconditional love for others.

Promise

He fulfils the desire of all who fear him,
  he also hears their cry, and saves them.
The Lord preserves all who love him;
  but all the wicked he will destroy.

Ps. 145:19-20, RSV

Prayer

Thank you, Lord, for blessing me when I
attempt to be of service to others. Amen.

Praise

May the nations be glad and sing for joy,
    because you judge the peoples
       with justice. . . .
May the peoples praise you, O God;
    may all the peoples praise you!

Ps. 67:4-5, TEV

Proposal

Why do you pass judgment on your brother
or sister? Or . . . despise [others]? For we will
all stand before the judgment seat of God.

Rom. 14:10, NRSV

Practice

Today I refuse to be a victim or take my
frustrations out on others. With the Lord by
my side, I shall overcome.

Promise

All these blessings shall come upon you and
overtake you, if you obey the voice of the
Lord your God.

Deut. 28:2, RSV

Prayer

Thank you, Lord, for speaking to me and
prodding my conscience. Amen.

December 21

Praise

Sing to him, sing praises to him,
    tell of all his wonderful works.
Glory in his holy name;
    let the hearts of those who seek the Lord
        rejoice.

1 Chron. 16:9-10, NRSV

Proposal

If I gave everything I have to poor people,
. . . but didn't love others, it would be of no
value whatever.

1 Cor. 13:3, TLB

Practice

Today I'll experience positive thinking by
remembering crises I've lived through and
handled successfully in the past.

Promise

Those who despise their neighbors
    are sinners, but
    happy are those who are kind to the poor.

Prov. 14:21, NRSV

Prayer

Thank you, Lord, for this day and strength
to handle what comes along. Amen.

Praise

I will tell of your name
    to my brothers and sisters;
    in the midst of the congregation
    I will praise you:
You who fear the Lord, praise him!

Ps. 22:22-23, NRSV

Proposal

Even if you should suffer for doing what is
right, how happy you are! Do not be afraid
of anyone, and do not worry.

1 Pet. 3:14, TEV

Practice

By the power of the Holy Spirit, today I'll
cast my worries into God's care.

Promise

With their mouths the godless
    would destroy their neighbors,
    but by knowledge the righteous
    are delivered.

Prov. 11:9, NRSV

Prayer

Thank you, Lord, for promoting peace in
me by delivering me from myself. Amen.

December 23

Praise

Always aim at those things that bring peace
and that help strengthen one another . . . so
that all of you together may praise with one
voice the God and Father of our Lord Jesus.

Rom. 14:19; 15:6, TEV

Proposal

This is the message which you have heard
from the beginning, that we should love
one another, and not be like Cain who was
of the evil one and murdered his brother.

1 John 3:11-12, RSV

Practice

Today I'll enthusiastically humble myself to
obey the Lord and be a blessing to others.

Promise

When you help the poor you are lending to
the Lord—and he pays wonderful interest
on your loan!

Prov. 19:17, TLB

Prayer

Thank you, Lord, for enabling me to look
beyond myself and be concerned for the
welfare of others. Amen.

December 24

Praise

I will give you thanks as long as I live;
    I will raise my hands to you in prayer. . . .
I will sing glad songs of praise to you.

Ps. 63:4-5, TEV

Proposal

Having purified your souls by your
obedience to the truth . . . love one another
earnestly from the heart.

1 Pet. 1:22, RSV

Practice

Today I'll make every effort to nurture personal relationships because people are
important to me and to my Lord.

Promise

If you are insulted because of the name of
Christ, you are blessed, for the Spirit of glory
and of God rests on you.

1 Pet. 4:14, NIV

Prayer

Thank you, Lord, for the spiritual blessings
that always result from suffering. Amen.

December 25

Praise

Suddenly a great army of heaven's angels appeared . . . singing praises to God:

"Glory to God in the highest heaven,
and peace on earth
to those with whom he is pleased!"

Luke 2:13-14, TEV

Proposal

Good news of great joy for all the people: to you is born this day in the city of David a Savior, who is the Messiah, the Lord.

Luke 2:10-11, NRSV

Practice

Today I'll rejoice for the life of my Master, the Lord Jesus Christ, Savior and Messiah.

Promise

The righteous shall move onward and forward; those with pure hearts shall become stronger and stronger.

Job 17:9, TLB

Prayer

Thank you, Lord, for the great joy of salvation which you offer to the whole world through Jesus. Amen.

December 26

Praise

His tongue was loosed, and he began to
speak, praising God . . .

"Praise be to the Lord, the God of Israel,
because he has come
and has redeemed his people."

Luke 1:64, 68, NIV

Proposal

Let no one despise your youth, but set the
believers an example in speech and conduct, in love, in faith, in purity.

1 Tim. 4:12, RSV

Practice

Today I'll establish high goals and depend
on hard work and the power of God's Spirit
to help me achieve them.

Promise

Those who lead many to righteousness,
[shall shine] like the stars forever and ever.

Dan. 12:3, NRSV

Prayer

Thank you, Lord, for the spiritual blessings
I've received from sharing with others.
Amen.

December 27

Praise

My eyes have seen your salvation,
   which you have prepared
      in the presence of all peoples,
a light for revelation to the Gentiles
   and for glory to your people Israel.

Luke 2:30-32, NRSV

Proposal

When there is jealousy among you and you
quarrel with one another, doesn't this prove
that you belong to this world?

1 Cor. 3:3, TEV

Practice

Today, instead of giving in to worldly strife,
I'll think about believers being God's
temple, with God's Spirit living within us.

Promise

Give heed to my reproof;
   behold, I will pour out my thoughts to you;
      I will make my words known to you.

Prov. 1:23, RSV

Prayer

Thank you, Lord, for reducing my desire to
be popular or the center of my life. Amen.

December 28

Praise

You servants of the Lord, praise his name!
. . . From the east to the west
      praise the name of the Lord!

Ps. 113:1, 3, TEV

Proposal

When they bring you to trial . . . do not
worry beforehand . . . but say whatever is
given you at that time, for it is not you who
speak, but the Holy Spirit.

Mark 13:11, NRSV

Practice

I refuse to allow the insensitivities and pet-
tiness of certain people to affect my attitude
toward folks in general.

Promise

There is deceit in the hearts
    of those who plot evil,
  but joy for those who promote peace.

Prov. 12:20, NIV

Prayer

Thank you, Lord, for releasing me from the
bondage of holding grudges and freeing
me to speak a gentle word of hope. Amen.

December 29

Praise

I have complete confidence, O God;
   I will sing and praise you! . . .
I will praise you among the peoples.

Ps. 57:7, 9, TEV

Proposal

Pay all your debts except the debt of love for
others—never finish paying that!

Rom. 13:8, TLB

Practice

Today I'll denounce the false god of human
perfection, and I'll embrace myself as God
has created and transformed me, a fallible,
forgiven human being.

Promise

The good obtain favor from the Lord,
   but those who devise evil he condemns.

Prov. 12:2, NRSV

Prayer

Thank you, Lord, for your saving mercy, for
accepting my joyful response of good
works, and for *not* demanding that I earn
salvation. Amen.

December 30

Praise

We give thanks to you, O God,
   we give thanks, for your Name is near.
. . . I will declare this forever;
   I will sing praise to the God of Jacob.

Ps. 75:1, 9, NIV

Proposal

We put aside all secret and shameful deeds.
. . . In the full light of truth we live in God's
sight and try to commend ourselves to
everyone's good conscience.

2 Cor. 4:2, TEV

Practice

Today I'll release my doubt, give up my
dependence on unworthy would-be
masters, and place my trust solely in Christ.

Promise

The blameless will have a goodly
inheritance.

Prov. 28:10, NRSV

Prayer

Thank you, Lord, for the fun that refreshes
when everything gets too serious. Amen.

December 31

Praise

I will praise you among the Gentiles. . . .
Praise the Lord, all you Gentiles,
    and sing praises to him, all you peoples.

Rom. 15:9, 11, NIV

Proposal

Let us therefore no longer pass judgment
on one another, but resolve instead never
to put a stumbling block or hindrance in the
way of another.

Rom. 14:13, NRSV

Practice

Today, instead of blaming others and
making excuses, I'll accept responsibility
for my actions and admit when I'm wrong.

Promise

To [God] who by the power at work within
us is able to accomplish abundantly far
more than all we can ask or imagine, to him
be glory . . . , forever and ever. Amen.

Eph. 3:20-21, NRSV

Prayer

Thank you, Lord, for joy that wells up within
when I trust you and help others. Amen.

*Be careful
how you think;
your life is shaped
by your thoughts.*

—Proverbs 4:23, TEV

*Blessed are
the pure in heart:
for they shall see God.*

—Matthew 5:8, KJV

The Author

L arry W. Wilson was born in Benwood, West Virginia, and lived with his grandparents in South Charleston. After high school and four years in the air force, he earned degrees in education and in counseling at Marshall University, Huntington, W. Va.

Wilson became a Christian, took seminary, and then earned a doctor of ministry degree while pastoring churches in the Western Pennsylvania Conference of the United Methodist Church.

Larry's wife is Shirley Kern Wilson, a native of Lancaster, Ohio. They have two children, Sarah and Michael, and live on rural route 1, Coal Center, Pa. 15423, where Larry pastors the Grace United Methodist Church (telephone number, 412 483-4448).

Notes